Lisa Cornwell is a priest in the Church
pleted a curacy in Newport Pagnell, she
Crowthorne, in Berkshire. Prior to ordination she was Head of
Religious Education at Newlands Girls' School in Maidenhead.
During her ministerial training she undertook a research project
for a Pastoral Theology MA module on the function of dreams for
furthering understanding of self and God, and she has also trained
in Spiritual Direction on the Ignatian Spirituality Course in London.
She is married to Mike, a primary school teacher.

DREAMS

DREAMS

The Path to Wholeness

LISA CORNWELL

First published in Great Britain in 2006

Society for Promoting Christian Knowledge
36 Causton Street
London SW1P 4ST

British Library Cataloguing-in-Publication Data
A catalogue record for this book is available from the British Library

ISBN-13: 978–0–281–05796–2
ISBN-10: 0–281–05796–6

1 3 5 7 9 10 8 6 4 2

Typeset by Graphicraft Ltd., Hong Kong
Printed in Great Britain by Ashford Colour Press

Contents

Prologue

After darkness falls
and duvet calls,
I drift into another realm
over which consciousness
surrenders control.
The deep sea of the unconscious
swells and floods
my beleaguered mind.
I am awash with plots, scenery
and symbols that defy logic.
Events that thrill and terrify.
Magical myths and mysteries.
Time knows no bounds;
I am a traveller through the planes
of personal and ancestral history.
I am subject. I am object.
I am actor. I am observer.
The drama is played out
on the stage of my mind.
Some characters familiar
others strangers, hidden behind
the mask of my persona.
What buried treasures and skeletons
will be uncovered
if I dare to delve
into my lost Atlantis?
– To recover of my sunken Self.

Foreword

Nightly we stand before the Magic Mirror of the Dream Which Never Lies.[1]

We've all had dreams that we feel are in some way speaking to us, and whether we feel amused, confused, embarrassed or downright alarmed, we may wish that we had some techniques and understanding to begin to fathom their significance. The aim of this book is to assist in that endeavour.

As an Anglican priest, I write unashamedly from a Christian perspective. However, this book is not aimed exclusively at a Christian readership. My hope is that it will be of interest to people from any religious disposition or none. I have assumed an interrogative approach to theology and psychology, which respects the integrity of each discipline. Psychology and theology are different ways of knowing; they inform and critique one another. Furthermore, 'although our perspectives on truth may be limited, partial and provisional, all truth is nevertheless God's truth'.[2]

A little self-knowledge can transform the way in which we relate to ourselves, the world and our Creator. *Dreams: The Path to Wholeness* seeks to demonstrate the relevance of dreams for both psychological and spiritual growth. Working with dreams is a lifetime's venture and one which we can primarily undertake on our own, but it also enhances the task of counselling and spiritual direction.

Permission has been granted for all the dream accounts included. To preserve confidentiality and anonymity, with the exception of family members stated, I have either avoided the use of names of people and places or employed pseudonyms where appropriate.

Lisa Cornwell

Acknowledgements

I would like to thank all those who have encouraged and inspired me on this path: those who have worked with me on my own dreams, those who have shared their dreams with me and permitted me to use them in this book, my editor Gordon Lamont for all his constructive comment, and last but not least, my husband Mike for his patience while I have been glued to my desk.

1

Our secret story

I am being chased relentlessly by an unknown man down the stair-well of a disused concrete block of flats. I shove the doors leading off from the stairs in turn but they are all locked. I continue to push through the fire doors on the stairs, pulling them shut behind me. I feel panic-stricken, desperate to escape the man hot on my heels.

As I near the bottom of the stairs I arrive at a side door that I can at last open. I burst through. A familiar woman is sitting inside on a red couch with her back to me. She turns to face me and I yell at her to bolt the door while I phone the police. I dash over to the tele-phone in the corner of the room and dial 999 but the operator tells me to call another number involving 6s and 7s. The woman is con-cerned for me. I am breathless and shaking but in control. I dial the new number.

Then I woke up.

Ah! Those four reassuring words 'then I woke up'! It was only a dream – thank God, it was only a dream! I am safe! But are we really safe as we haul ourselves into consciousness and throw ourselves into the rigours of the day to forget the horrors of the night? We may well be safe from the immediate danger presented in the dream, but the dream itself is in fact calling attention to a deeper reality. The dream is offering us a truth about ourselves. When we are disturbed by troublesome dreams, the danger that presents itself in symbolic form still remains in real life. We are not 'safe' after all. The dream acts as a warning. It may take some work to unravel what it actually represents, but we ignore the dream at our own peril. Most of us spend our conscious lives rushing from one activity to the next. We are not accustomed to listening to ourselves – our own minds and bodies. While our bodies are in slumber, our brains are still active and we become a captive audience for our inner concerns. I believe that dreams, far from being meaningless sojourns of the soul or the recycling of neural waste, are a powerful communication from our-selves to ourselves; and this belief will be explored in this book. For many people, dream images, if remembered, will be hastily shrugged off with the duvet. However, for those who dare to take the lid off the dream experience and delve a little deeper, the outcome can be life-changing. To grapple with our dreams is to embark upon a life-long process of 'Self' discovery.

The psychological structure of the Self

We will return to the opening dream account later in this chapter. First, it will be helpful to define the term 'Self', drawing upon the language of psychology. The 'Self' denotes the whole person, but there is more to us than meets the eye. To understand the structure of the Self, we turn to the insights of Carl Gustav Jung (1875–1961). When speaking of the mind and mental activity Jung uses the terms 'psyche' and 'psychic' in order to cover both the conscious and the unconscious.[1] Jung's model of the psyche can be likened to an island. The conscious part is the land seen above the water but by far the greatest portion of land lies unknown beneath the surface.[2] The Self consists of the following:

The conscious or public Self (the Persona)

This is the 'us' that the world sees and how we perceive ourselves. The 'ego' is the knowing, willing 'I' centre of consciousness. What belongs to consciousness is not fully conscious all the time. In order to conduct our lives we need to suppress thoughts and information surplus to requirements at the time. *Suppression* is 'the necessary withdrawal of attention from some things so that we can attend to others, but in this case they can be recalled at will'.[3]

The personal unconscious (the Shadow)

This is the repressed Self, which also includes forgotten experiences and subliminal perceptions that don't reach consciousness – we do not become fully aware of much of what we experience. *Repression* is 'the deliberate and continuous withdrawal of attention, so that the thought, feeling, event, which is to be repressed is at least expelled from consciousness and we are unable to recall it'.[4] (Note the distinction from 'suppression'.) This is a 'shadow land stretching between the ego and the unconscious . . . a land which has not always been covered by the sea, and can be reclaimed'.[5] During sleep, memories of the personal unconscious may return of their own accord as repression weakens.

The collective unconscious

This is a deeper level of the unconscious. The brain is shaped by inherited human experience.[6] The collective unconscious is a repository of 'archetypes', described by Jung as 'primordial types, that is, with universal images that have existed since the remotest times'.[7] We are part of something much bigger than ourselves. This is borne out by the various figures that recur in dreams and fantasies which correlate with historical parallels and universal myths. At the heart of the collective unconscious is the 'Self', i.e. the *whole* person, including unrealized potential and unconscious contents.

The human Shadow

Following this model, 'what you see' is certainly not 'what you get'. We are rather complicated beings. At birth our conscious and unconscious Selves are not so highly differentiated. In the course of growing up, we repress aspects of our personalities which we feel are unacceptable to our family and other authority figures. These rejected and subsequently inaccessible aspects of the Self make up what Jung called the 'shadow complex'.[8]

> The shadow possesses qualities that the superego (the internalized parental authority) loathes and despises: normally one denies these qualities in oneself, preferring to project them unconsciously outside on to those whom one perceives as socially undesirable.[9]

Thus, the Shadow is that primitive instinctive side of ourselves that we may be taught to deny as we grow up. Yet denying its existence does not destroy it. In *A Little Book of the Human Shadow*, Robert Bly describes the personal Shadow as 'the long bag we drag behind us'. It is as though we have had an invisible bag behind us since infancy. As we have gone through life, the parts of us our parents, teachers and significant others disapproved of have got stuffed into the bag. Bly recalls that 'By the time my brother and I were twelve in Madison, Minnesota . . . our bags were already a mile long.'[10]

Culture and religion will further dictate the items that get put in the bag. Within this, images of God presented and perceived are significant. If we try to live up to the standards of a God who is purely light, then we will be unable to handle the darkness within us. If we cannot handle it we repress it. But the more we repress it, the more it leads its own life because it is not integrated.[11] We may convince ourselves that we have safely buried our Shadow Selves out of sight and mind, leaving us to present a respectable Persona to the rest of the world, but in actual fact the Shadow may not remain so compliant. We run the risk of becoming split into two people, one conscious and one unconscious. This is wonderfully illustrated by the classic tale of *The Strange Case of Dr Jekyll and Mr Hyde*. It is notable that Stevenson gained his original inspiration for the work through a dream.[12] Dr Jekyll is a man who is the paragon of respectability in Victorian bourgeois society. Being seen to be morally virtuous and having the right etiquette was paramount. However, Jekyll recognized that a lifetime of denying his baser passions would be intolerable. He conceived the person of Mr Hyde in order to give his instinctive Self free reign, while keeping the reputation of Dr Jekyll untarnished. Thus, he lived the double life as Jekyll and Hyde – good versus evil.

The Shadow is not evil in itself. However, it has the potential for evil when it is left unharnessed or, perhaps worse still, unacknowledged. When the undeveloped, under-exercised Shadow side of the personality is set free by itself, it leads ultimately to destruction. This same theme is played out in William Golding's *Lord of the Flies*. When a group of schoolboys find themselves stranded on a desert island without the restraint of the adult 'civilized' world, it does not take long for 'the beast' within the boys to emerge. In both stories, those who set themselves free from moral restraint become ruled by evil, which is to become sub-human. Human history testifies to instances in which the collective Shadow has erupted in a nation. Initially it boasts actions which are for the good of human civilization, and then the horrors of evil become apparent to those without blinkers. Hitler's Nazi Germany is a typical example. There are others, and we can never be so complacent as to imagine that history will not repeat itself in different guises. John Sanford puts it starkly: 'The shadow, feared and rejected, becomes evil . . . today we all stand in fear of one thing: that our unrecognised, unredeemed shadow will start another frightful catastrophe. We all talk of peace but prepare for war.'[13]

The Christian tradition, under the influence of Greek thought, has tended to polarize light and dark into good and evil. The latter is to be shunned and overcome. On a macro level, this rationale has led to atrocities in the name of religion, such as the Crusades. Even today this 'God is on our side' mentality is used as a justification for war which does not meet the classical 'Just War' criteria.[14] Such language was used by President Bush to further the cause of the Iraq war. He couched it in terms of 'good versus evil', the rationale being that the 'good' West would overcome the evildoers who threatened the civilized world. This thinking negates the dark drives within us that need to be identified. According to the *Church Times*, 'An independent Washington think-tank, the Middle East Research and Information Project, has pointed out that control of Iraq would give the US a base at the heart of the world's largest oil reserves.'[15] Perhaps the President's motives were not so pure after all. The Bishop of Durham, Dr Tom Wright, described President Bush and Mr Blair as people who 'still invoke Jesus to support plans that look much more like those of [the Roman Emperor] Augustus'.[16]

A Christian perspective should not paint God's intentions in such black-and-white terms. Life is full of complexity. God is revealed in the life of Jesus Christ. Jesus lived with tension and embraced darkness. The temptation of Christ in the wilderness was a defining moment. Why did Jesus go into the wilderness following his baptism? Mark's Gospel is clear: 'the Spirit immediately drove him out into the wilderness' (Mark 1.12).[17] Jesus went into the wilderness because God's Spirit *impelled* him to go there! Jesus was not lured into the wilderness by Satan but driven there by God so that he might face and conquer the temptations involved in his calling as Messiah before commencing his ministry. Jesus remained in the solitude of the wilderness for forty days, which echoes the forty years of testing that Israel also endured in the wilderness. The wilderness was seen as a gloomy place of terror, the abode of devils and unclean beasts. But Jesus was not completely abandoned by God – he was not beyond the bounds of God's love. He still remains the 'beloved Son'. There is the reassurance of 'angels'. Yet this wilderness environment was also symbolic of a deeper struggle. During this time, Christ had to come face to face with his inner wilderness, the darkness within – all the doubts and fears that may have been lurking there about his own identity and the task ahead of him. Whether or not you believe in a literal Devil is irrelevant in this respect. Jesus had to face the demons within.

Jesus' teaching, 'Be perfect as your heavenly Father is perfect', is not the perfection of suppressing the darkness, but the perfection of integrated wholeness.[18] For Jesus the biggest challenge ahead was at the end of his earthly ministry. Again there was the temptation to take the easy way out, but Christ remained true to his calling. At the moment of his death, Christ embraced the darkness of alienation from God the Father. Yet God's reality embraces the one who cries out, 'My God, my God, why have you forsaken me?' and dies; then everything is embraced – life and death.[19]

There is a strand within the Christian tradition, known as apophatic theology, that has tended to be neglected in the West. It emphasizes the unknowability of God. This is not to say that God cannot be known, but that God in himself cannot be understood. It is the negative way. We can only speak of what God is not. It is the opposite of cataphatic theology (that which is 'known'). Apophatic theology goes beyond language and discursive theology and seeks union with God through a prayer that is stripped of all images and words. It is difficult to identify an origin to apophatic theology. It may have originally been influenced by Platonic thought. It is an integral part of Eastern Orthodoxy and is evident in the writings of some of the early Church Fathers.

Gregory of Nyssa taught that God is incomprehensible to humans, not because of fallen human nature but because of God's very essence. Humans must go through the way of negation, a process of elimination of what God is not. He hypothesized that, first, there is some *light* – some illumination of the soul – in order to restore the image of God. This is followed by a struggle. As the soul progresses in the knowledge of God, it becomes aware of the utter transcendence of God and that God is essentially hidden and incomprehensible – the God of the *cloud*. The third stage is the stage of *darkness*, whereby it is realized that God dwells in darkness and that the search for God is the search for the one who is hidden. God is found in the obscurity of faith.

The darkness is due to a lack of knowing because of the brightness of the light. It is impossible to look at the sun without being blinded; so, with God, the light of faith overwhelms the light of the intellect. The unknown author of the classic *The Cloud of*

Unknowing[20] writes, 'By love he may be sought and held, but not by thought.'[21] The author offers the following guidance:

> When you first begin, you may find only darkness – a cloud of unknowing, as it were. It will seem incomprehensible, meaningless, except that in your innermost will you will feel a simple steadfast intention reaching out towards God. No matter what you do, this darkness, this cloud, will seem to remain between you and God. It will stop you seeing God in the clear light of rational understanding and from experiencing his loving mercy in your inner being. But be reconciled to the fact that you must wait in this darkness as long as necessary, and don't give up. Continue to struggle, longing to know God whom you love. For if you are ever to feel him and see him in this life, it will always be in this darkness, this cloud.[22]

Apophatic theology has also influenced Christian mystics, such as St John of the Cross, Julian of Norwich and, more latterly, Thomas Merton. As the author of the *Cloud* makes plain, it is a discipline that requires a certain amount of patience. Maybe, apart from our love of certainties, that is why we have avoided this spirituality in the West. To encounter God as mystery helps us to embrace the mystery of ourselves. When we let go of our tight grip on God and on ourselves, truth begins to unfold itself. What is 'dark' is what is hidden or not known. The Shadow is the dark side of us that is concealed from the light. It needs to be brought out into the open. The image of a shadow is a helpful visual one because we see it is the area where the sun's access is blocked. We need to allow the sun's rays to illuminate those parts of ourselves that are in shadow – not so that they vanish but so that they can be integrated within our personalities. This is by no means a straightforward process. Stevens observes:

> The hidden shadow qualities are commonly concealed behind the persona, the actor's 'mask' of social adaptation we put on when we go out to meet the world. The more guilty or insecure we are about the shadow, the more prone we are to develop a persona whose *raison d'être* is to disguise, to camouflage, and to deceive.[23]

This is where dreams are invaluable, for dreams do not lie. Dreams compensate our conscious distorted picture of ourselves by revealing our Shadow. Dreams act as the sun's rays showing our nature in its true light. When the Shadow is denied in waking life, we may be threatened by 'Shadow dreams'. Such dreams present uncomfortable issues which we normally choose not to face.[24] They have the purpose of awakening us to the unacceptable aspects of ourselves that we repress for fear of losing status or suffering rejection. The Shadow is often represented by dream characters 'who pursue us past every obstacle, and into the blind alleyways and eerie basements of the mind'.[25] The dream account at the beginning of this chapter, which we will now give the title 'The Chase', can be regarded as a typical Shadow dream.

This dream occurred at a point in my life when my Persona felt under threat, a time of transition and change in my life. Previously I had been secure in my professional identity as a teacher. However, when I had to leave this behind to live as a student in training for the ministry I found myself in a curious state of limbo, being neither one thing nor the other. The condition of being 'de-skilled' stripped me of my defences to come face to face with my raw Self. Of course I still remained a qualified teacher, and that will always be a part of me, but I could no longer be defined by that. It left me grappling with the essence of who I was. Before ordination, the best advice I was given was 'be yourself', and by then I understood why. Now my identity is bound up with being a priest, but that is not a mask that I wear: it is integrated with my personality, my very being.

How, in brief, did the dream facilitate this realization? At this stage, I will offer up an interpretation without enlarging upon the process as this will be addressed later in the book. The following conclusions took some time to crystallize. The building is a symbol of my 'Self'. As I run down the stairwell I am going down into my own depths. The locked rooms are the inaccessible parts of my Self that I have unconsciously shut off. It is significant that I did arrive at the bottom and there I found a safe place. It is possible that the woman on the couch represents both who she is in real life and that aspect of myself – how I perceived her. An incident in life involving her acted as a catalyst to raise my insecurities. It is interesting that the couch was red; on the one hand it spells danger, but on the other it has womb-like associations which connect with the room being a safe hidden place. The attempt at dialling '999' and instead being instructed to dial 6s and 7s turns it into a pun on 'being at sixes and sevens'. Dreams have a wonderful way of throwing up puns! It finally dawned upon me that my pursuer was the archetype of the Shadow, representing the aspects of my Self that I had repressed or ignored.

Instead of facing my attacker, I ran away and called for the door to be bolted against him. The 'threat' still lurks outside.

The Shadow arouses in us strong emotions of fear, anger and moral outrage. Stevens explains,

> At the core of the shadow complex is the archetype of the Enemy. Learning to live on good terms with 'the enemy within' means that one is less likely to project it on to other people . . . instead of controlling (repressing) it or running away from it (denial), the ego initiates dialogue with the shadow, and, by confronting it and making efforts to befriend it, enters into a hedonic bond with it, thus rendering its energy available to the total personality.[26]

In the context of my dream, it would have been interesting to have seen how my 'aggressor' would have reacted if my ego, the 'I' part of me, had stopped to confront him and maybe asked him what he wanted! Sanford testifies to instances where people have been able to take such action in a dream, and commonly a reconciliation between the parties takes place.[27] Stevens concurs:

> When . . . the shadow is acknowledged and 'owned', an important change comes over the personality as a whole: not only do we stop running away from our own aggressiveness, but we take possession of it, assume responsibility for it, and use it, one hopes, *ethically*.[28]

Although the Shadow is usually experienced as dangerous and hostile, not all Shadow dreams are of the 'fight or flight' variety. Shadow characters appear as our opposites, personifying the character traits that we have neglected. Thus, the timid man may dream of an assertive character and so on. The rejected parts of the personality may be felt to be negative but they emerge in dreams with a positive end in mind. They have been 'left out in the cold' to our own detriment. We are faced with them in order to embrace them and bring about greater equilibrium in our lives.

The 'Chase' dream was only a beginning, one step on the journey to self-discovery, simply a bringing to awareness of the need to recognize the Shadow side of myself. It does not stop there. Bly concluded, 'We spend our life until we're twenty deciding what parts of ourself to put into the bag, and we spend the rest of our lives trying to get them out again.'[29] This can be a painful but nonetheless rewarding process. 'To suffer the guilt, shame, despair, and anxiety of restoring them to consciousness is to take the first step towards wholeness.'[30] When we take ownership of our entire Selves, we embark on a life-long process of self-discovery. The following dream account is a continuation along that path.

The dark path

Scene 1

I am in an unknown house with various people. I think there is a bedroom with bunk beds in it and I also enter a kitchen. I do not know what the occasion is.

Scene 2

I am in a reasonably crowded swimming pool. I think my fiancé and one of my close friends are here. I do not appear to be swimming laps, as I would usually do in reality, but just dipping in and out of the water. Another woman, whom I don't know, is prominent. I carry out some sort of personal survival exercise with her in the pool. I'm not sure who is saving whom.

Scene 3

I am walking with my friend (same as scene 2) along a path bordering the Moody housing estate in Bovingdon, where we both used to live in our latter childhood and teenage years. Initially, we are in the Hyde Lane section and then the path joins up with the rougher, more secluded cut-through to the other side of the village. Strangely, the gate through to this second path has been moved further down so that there is a new stretch in between. It all appears a little different to me since I was here last but my friend knows about this alteration. We walk a little further on and the path forks into two parallel paths separated by scrub bushes and trees. The path to the left is called the 'black' (or 'dark'?) path, as opposed to the 'light' path on the right. Without hesitation we continue down the path on the left.

Shortly, we find ourselves in a room with cupboard doors around the walls. The doors become like the cases that contain Egyptian mummies. There is a sinister atmosphere in the room but I don't feel particularly afraid. One or two of the doors are opened and there are mummy-like creatures inside, but without the bandages! They have the appearance of Egyptian gods with animal heads. The creatures step out and we/I have to take their place behind the doors. It turns into some sort of machine and I have to undergo a process that will bring my inner dark side to the surface. I feel myself being churned up, almost like being put through a non life-threatening electric current or in a food blender. It is some sort of ritual purification. The dream ends before the process is complete.

This was an immensely powerful, 'master' dream that has taken months to unravel. The associations are manifold: by no means can full justice be done to the dream in a few paragraphs, but the following insights will suffice to give a 'feel' for the dream and its purpose. The scenes are connected and each scene goes deeper. Scene 1 uses everyday images, although at the outset it appears to be somewhat superficial and vague. Scene 2 reaches further into the personal unconscious. It is more symbolic and obscure. Scene 3 goes even deeper into the unconscious and also taps into the collective unconscious, speaking the language of archetypes. It journeys back through time in terms of both my personal and ancestral history.

Scene 1 is a prelude to the rest: it sets the scene. A house is a symbol of the psyche. I am in an 'unknown house', in other words an unknown part of myself. This was true of my life situation – I was in the first year of parish ministry as a deacon before being ordained priest and also preparing for my own marriage – a great time of upheaval and transition. I was in uncharted territory. The various people are the various parts of myself that I don't recognize in this place. The house is not described in full but, with the exception of a bathroom, the basic rooms are in place. The kitchen is a place of transformation and nourishment, where raw materials can become nutritious and appetizing meals. The bedroom is the most private room in the house, a secret place that a person can retire to. It is also a place of intimacy.

The water in Scene 2 is symbolic of my unconscious Self. I am 'dipping in and out of the water'. It mirrored my life situation of not yet being 'fully in the swim' but being determined to survive and learn how to survive. The other woman is that aspect of myself who knows how to survive and help others. The male aspect of myself in the form of my fiancé and my inner companion in the form of my close friend lend support in the situation. The fact that I am able to dip into my unconscious Self and still survive serves as a bridge to the next scene.

In the quest to identify the dark, i.e. Shadow, side of myself, I am taken back to the scene of my youth in Scene 3. This is unsurprising considering how the Shadow is formed. Once again, I am accompanied by the reassuring presence of my inner companion. She is the part of me that does 'know' and enables me to feel safe. There is an interesting play on place names. The 'Moody' estate has associations of teenage moodiness and with Hyde Lane the tale of *Dr Jekyll and Mr Hyde* springs to mind – a highly significant pun in view of what follows. The path turns out not to be quite the same path as I thought it would be, just as my current path in life is maybe not the path I would have foreseen. The path forks into two parallel paths. A choice must be made between them but there is no need for discernment; the unerring instinct is to continue down the path on the left, the 'black' or 'dark' path. This is contrary to the popular light–dark duality in Christian consciousness. In the dream, what is black or dark is that which is unknown or mysterious as opposed to the enlightenment of light. I am brought back into the world of those earlier years of my life at a time of maturity in my psyche when I am ready to go down that black path. It is a soul journey.

The room with cupboard doors symbolizes the place in myself where lots of things are put in cupboards. It links with the unknown house of Scene 1. Doors reveal what we really are. The dream is inviting me to go back into that old place where things are put away in cupboards. It raises the question: what were the aspects of me that became repressed during that phase of my life? That is the challenge of the dream and my ongoing task to discover. The Egyptian mummy creatures are there to facilitate the process. The fact that the bandages are missing indicates that 'Mummy' now needs to be unwrapped, as in the dream. It has the potential to be interpreted on different levels. On one level, there is my own 'Mummy' and corresponding childhood associations. Then there is the archetypal level of the Egyptian gods. Upon reflection, it was the jackal-headed god that was key. This is Anubis, the god that takes people from life into the underworld (death), but there they come alive. In my professional life I also conduct religious rituals, of which funerals are the most awesome – I stand in the shoes of Anubis. Death and resurrection is a central theme in Christian thought, not only in the sense of our final destiny but during our earthly life, in the sense of 'dying to self' and finding one's true Self. The dream takes me into the heart of mysterious religious ritual. The machine that will 'bring my dark side to the surface' is about a life task and a spiritual task. It is not an instant or straightforward process. It is uncomfortable but it is not life-threatening. The situation does not destroy me. The purpose of the dream is for me to claim and integrate my Shadow in order to bring about wholeness. The end of the dream is where the energy of the dream and the psyche wants to take me for new life.

Integrating the Self – individuation

Jung employed the term *individuation* to describe the process 'by which every living organism becomes what it was destined to become from the beginning'.[31] Individuation takes place in the second half of life when the true Self emerges, like the rising sun, above the fragmented unconscious and Persona. It involves reintegration of our whole personality so as to become a more complete person. Stevens observes, 'It is characteristic of the individuation process that the shadow should evidently wish to abandon its outsider status and *intrude* – i.e. gain entrance to the conscious personality in order to promote wholeness.'[32]

In the opening dream account, the threatening Shadow stayed locked outside the room. I thought I was 'safe', but little did I know that the Shadow eventually finds a way to break in uninvited. This occurred over two years later in another lengthy dream. I will simply illustrate the point with the relevant section. To put the scene in context, in the dream I have checked into hospital to have an operation. I start to have doubts about whether I have been assigned the right bed:

> There is another bed in a different wing of the hospital that I think I should be in. The nurse takes me over there with my belongings. It turns out to be a very small ward in an alcove, containing two beds pushed up together. There is a man called Ian in one of them, but then to my distress I discover that he is the tramp who has recently started sleeping in the porch of a village church where I take services. I certainly do not want him to see and recognize me in this context. I want to remain anonymous. He rolls over and pokes his head out of the covers. Hurriedly, I zip up my jacket around my face and scuttle out. I explain to the nurse who he is and what my role is and why I couldn't be in the bed right next to him. She is understanding. It transpires that he broke into the hospital through a window to get a bed for the night. There isn't actually anything wrong with him.

The 'tramp' feels threatening. He is rough, lazy and unclean. I am very wary of him. He is my opposite, my Shadow Self, that I recoil from. My anxiety is unwarranted as he is harmless in the dream. I need to learn to lose my fear and make friends with him. My purpose for being in the hospital is to have an operation. To befriend the Shadow would be a significant step towards healing and wholeness. The dream continues but the operation does not take place before it ends. Nonetheless, this is a significant step forward from the earlier dream. Although I haven't exactly welcomed him with open arms, my Shadow has gained entrance. This reflects my conscious desire to identify my Shadow in order to be a more integrated person.

Global individuation

It is unsurprising that, in our socio-historical context, we should experience ourselves as part-personalities. The Age of Enlightenment rejected the old certainties of the Judaeo-Christian tradition in favour of a quest for absolute knowledge through human rationality, initiated by Descartes's famous axiom, *Cogito ergo sum*, 'I think therefore I am'. However, two world wars and the horrors of the Holocaust and Hiroshima shattered this unswerving optimistic pride in human achievement and technological progress. Anti-modernist movements, opposed to institutionalized power, arose in the 1960s, leading to the emergence of postmodernism as a movement between 1968 and 1972.[33] The influential French postmodern philosopher Jean-François Lyotard characterizes the postmodern condition as incredulity towards 'meta-narratives' (any universal story or truth claim which attempts to make sense of the world). He asserts that meta-narratives are relative to times and places and must be deconstructed. As such, both modernity and postmodernity remained rooted in the Cartesian hermeneutic of suspicion, be it of religious or of secular beliefs. The starting premise is one of disillusionment.

Contemporary Western society is characterized by fragmentation. The postmodern legacy is that relativism rules. Truth is a matter of consumer preference. This philosophy has filtered into our understanding of our very identities. We are what we construct ourselves to be. I may be one person at work and another at home. In the world of the media, image is all-important and the latest is best. Pop stars need to constantly re-invent themselves in order to retain their credibility. Take Madonna, for example! The rather alarming consequence of all this is that, as a society, not only have we lost our sense of past and future but we have become largely divorced from our collective unconscious and the *Imago Dei*, God-image, imprinted within each of us. We are fragmented, cut adrift in a sea of uncertainty. Soulless modernist rationalism has meant that the arts have become progressively secular, stripped of all mythic reference and spiritual wonder. Hence, the only place left for these values is the world of dreams.[34]

> What myths, ritual, and dreams do is integrate the systems of which the mind–brain is composed. What Western culture has achieved is their separation . . . Before the Enlightenment, ego, Self, community, and cosmos were experienced as more closely linked because religion *yoked* them together.[35]

In the same way as we recognize the significance of the individual individuation process, we can work towards collective individuation both locally and globally. Just as individuals can repress their own Shadow and project it on to others, so too do whole nations. We need to rediscover and integrate the lost aspects of our heritage, our spiritual roots and connectedness, otherwise we are in danger of self-destruction, be it through warfare or ecological disaster. This involves re-uniting our right brain hemispheres with the logical left hemispheres. Increasing self-awareness of what has previously remained unconscious or denied is the first step towards transforming society. To give time and energy to dreams, therefore, is not self-indulgent navel-gazing, but a spiritual duty of cultural and ecological significance: the more conscious we become as individuals, the more hope there is for our planet.[36]

Amid the cultural disintegration, there exists a desperate search for wholeness, a yearning for unity and a desire to discover the interconnectedness of all things. Madonna, to resume the example, has become an adherent of cabbala (Jewish mysticism) in a quest for spiritual enlightenment and self-improvement. Many celebrities, in keeping with the postmodern mindset, are pick and mixing from the smorgasbord of spiritual wares on offer, in the search for personal fulfilment. Sometimes this extends to the transcendent dimension, however that is recognized. The search for God and the search for self-realization can be synonymous.

Self-knowledge and God-knowledge

Both self-knowledge and God-knowledge are forms of 'religious knowing' – religious knowledge which surpasses mere 'head' knowledge. Religious cognition is not simply an assent to a set of prescribed beliefs but contains an emotional component and involves personal transformation. In *The Psychology of Religious Knowing*, Fraser Watts and Mark Williams aim to relate religious knowing to cognitive psychology. They maintain that religious knowledge is reached by cognitive processes; this can entail a sudden insight but ordinarily takes time and effort. They propose a 'middle way' which charts a course between the extremes of pure faith and pure reason, between subjectivity and objectivity.[37] A distinction is made between cerebral knowing and a deeper intuitive knowing:

> One of the core features of the religious life is coming to *know* from direct experience what may previously have been a mere matter of religious teaching or of faith. This does not necessarily produce any changes in *what* is known though it may do so, but it changes very radically *how* it is known.[38]

Dreams are such a 'direct experience' for religious knowing. The doctrine of humanity as created in the image of God leads to the view, prominent in the writings of the contemplatives, that there is an element in human nature that is a reflection of God. The assumption is that there is an inner path that leads to God. Paul Tillich described God as the 'ground of our being'.[39] Thus, knowledge of Self through dreams leads to knowledge of God. As we grow in self-knowledge we may become aware that we are actually holding on to a distorted image of God. Ana-Maria Rizzuto advocates that the God representation is highly personalized and drawn from many sources. 'The entire representational process occurs in a wider context of the family, social class, organized religion, and particular subcultures.'[40] How we picture God is naturally bound up with our own life experiences. It is highly subjective and may say more about us than an external reality. R. W. Hood, on the other hand, argues that 'part of one's sense of God comes from God'.[41] Dreams can reveal to us not only our self-perception but also our perception of God. It is important that we do not just rely upon our conscious understanding of God and ourselves but allow our dreams to reveal the truth of God and ourselves to us. This is not to usurp a more cognitive approach. Subjective knowledge is not an alternative to biblical teaching; rather, it should interact with it. The Bible gives an account of God's involvement in human affairs over a large period of history and reveals the nature of God to us. Dreams feature widely, as we shall discover later on. Thus, Scripture, tradition, reason and personal experience are all to be taken into account. With sufficient self and theological insight our false images of God can be redeemed.

The psyche is inherently religious. The Self is connected with God or 'the transcendent'. Jung viewed the God-image as a symbol of the state of individuation, which led him increasingly to see the Self as an image of God.[42] Jung does not reject a transcendent concept of God but is preoccupied with his immanence: 'people will need to rediscover God through the archetype of God in their own unconscious'.[43] The following dream account is a remarkable example of this occurrence:

> I'm on the moon, or it might be Mars, at the main part of a base. I've come in from a secondary base ... Something is going wrong at the main base, it's a political thing and I'm part of some kind of rebellion. I shoot a hole in the main door and a leader from the main base who has challenged me can't believe what I have done. We put our hands around what is a perfectly round hole, six inches across. We can feel all the air rushing out and the base dies, everybody there dies. Now I'm on the second base and we're having to struggle for survival.
>
> And then there is a jump ... and I'm with my wife on Mars and we are climbing. The planet is being terra-formed and is becoming much more hospitable. I even saw a horse and carriage! We are on this incredible mountain range and the clouds very briefly part and high high high above us is the peak of Olympus Mons (the biggest mountain/volcano on Mars or in the solar system). It was absolutely breath-taking. It is the strongest emotion I have ever felt in a dream.

The dreamer had discussed this dream with his spiritual director and as a result a great deal emerged from it. He offers the following interpretation:

> The hole is important because it is perfectly round ... The air rushing out is important because it means I've left something behind ... and am moving on to where I belong ... I was very aware in the dream that I was going to Mars ... Venus is supposed to represent women and Mars is supposed to represent men. It's a man's planet ... This is the idea of the unconscious mind throwing puns ... Mars is about grown men and Mars is being terra-formed. It is probably an image of me – it is being made easier to live on, which is very encouraging! But *the* most important thing was the parting of the clouds and glimpsing, just for a moment, the peak and the feeling of it being absolutely awe-inspiringly breath-taking, the feeling of absolute rapture, and that apparently, in Jungian terms, is when you glimpse the Self – you glimpse the core person in a dream ... what you are looking at is so incredibly beautiful, and it really was!

This was an incredibly evocative and positive dream. Seeing the Self is a rare thing, and the dreamer awoke in a state of rapture. It was a religious experience. To quote Sanford, 'an experience with the Self is like an experience with God'.[44] This is not to infer that the Self *is* God. We ourselves are not divine; rather, we carry within each of us the divine image. The need remains to differentiate between God as a transcendent ultimate reality and God in his immanence, the 'God within'. However, there is a correspondence between them. Sanford is convinced that 'Through the God in the psyche there is mediated the will and energy of the Creator himself'.[45]

It is arguable that if God is the source of our being, then he is in our unconscious Selves and is the co-author of our dreams. Dreams stem from our own psychology but they are also a means of communication by God. This is not to suggest that God communicates in any special and revelatory way (although this has been known) but that God uses the normal production of dreams to awaken us to the pain and potential in our lives. Dreams 'express the mind of God within us'.[46] God shares the same goal as our own psyche: that is, our ultimate healing and wholeness.

There is a subtle but important distinction to be made between the centre of our conscious being, the ego, and the centre of total psyche, the Self. When the ego assumes a godlike role, the outcome can be disastrous.[47] This is illustrated by the story of the Fall in Genesis chapter 3. It contains a rueful truth about human nature that has been perpetuated throughout history. Instead, the ego was created to cultivate the aspirations of the larger personality within us. 'We are not masters but servants of the God within.'[48] Self-realization, therefore, is far bigger than realizing the limited and selfish purposes of the ego. Dreams reveal a meaning and purpose beyond ourselves and our conscious imaginings. From a Christian perspective, this entails our ongoing transformation into Christ's likeness. This means putting Christ at the centre of our lives in place of our own ego, so we can say in the words of St Paul, 'it is no longer I who live, but it is Christ who lives in me' (Galatians 2.20). Moreover, it is through our Christlike centre that our whole Self may be realized.[49]

Conclusion

During this life, we are all in process. St Paul continued to struggle with the reality of his own egotism and splintered Self, and so do we. The good news is that God embraces us as we are – light and shadow. That is grace. As we wrestle in our own depths with God and with our very Selves, Christ's light begins to shine through. Others may begin to see God in us, the God we may even fail to recognize in ourselves. As God is realized within us, our true and complete Selves are enabled to flourish. The dreams become reality.

I began in Eden,
    the Place of Promise,
    the Arena of Alienation.
Yahweh is walking in the garden.
He is so close
I could reach out and touch him.
But I hold back.
I am in hiding.
I have concealed my naked Self
    from God
    from my helpmate
    from the world.
Yahweh senses me crouching
bare behind the bushes,
summons me out
back to the source of life,
where he fashioned me out of the soil
and breathed the breath of life
into my nostrils.
The breath of liberty and love.
And I am no longer ashamed.

2

The dimensions of the dreamworld

To be or not to be: that is the question:
Whether 'tis nobler in the mind to suffer
The slings and arrows of outrageous fortune,
Or to take arms against a sea of troubles,
And by opposing end them?
To die: to sleep;
No more; and, by a sleep to say we end
The heart-ache and the thousand natural shocks
That flesh is heir to, 'tis a consummation
Devoutly to be wish'd. To die, to sleep;
To sleep: perchance to dream: ay, there's the rub:
For in that sleep of death what dreams may come.[1]

(Shakespeare's *Hamlet*)

Our need to dream

A night dream is a spontaneous symbolic experience lived out in the
inner world during sleep. Such dreams are composed of a series of
images, actions, thoughts, words, and feelings over which we seem to
have little or no conscious control.[2]

You may not *remember* your dreams but, believe me, you have them.
Dreaming is a fact of life. It is a biological necessity. A scientific interest in sleep patterns and dreaming emerged in the last century.
Research began in 1953 when an American, Nathaniel Kleitman, and
his student Eugene Aserinsky observed that the eyes of sleeping
infants and adults move about rapidly behind closed eyelids for
short periods. EEG readings, which record the electrical activity of
the brain, showed that these periods of eye movement correspond
with particular brain rhythms. This phase of sleep was termed REM
(Rapid Eye Movement) sleep. The discovery of a link between eye
movement and recognizable brain waves gave rise to the break-
through observation that REM sleep is associated with dreaming.[3]

Further research showed that periods of REM sleep regularly occur about every 90 minutes throughout the night, each episode persisting for a longer period of time from 10 to 40 minutes. During a typical night, sleep begins with the hypnagogic state, lasting several minutes, in which fragmented images and dramatic episodes are perceived in vivid clarity. This is followed by slow wave non-REM (NREM) deep-level sleep for about 90 minutes. Then comes the first REM stage of the night for about 10 minutes. The EEG readings become irregular in frequency and low in amplitude (as when awake). The second and third REM periods are of increasing duration and follow shorter NREM episodes. The final REM interval lasts up to 40 minutes and is usually followed by waking. If a dream is remembered it is usually from this last phase. Altogether, REM occupies about 25 per cent of each night's sleep. In theory, this means that a 75-year-old will have spent at least 50,000 hours – that is six years – dreaming![4]

During REM sleep brain activity, adrenaline levels, pulse rate and oxygen consumption come closest to those in wakefulness, yet muscle tone relaxes – the eye muscles appear to be the only ones that are physically involved in acting out dream events. When dreams are at their most vivid, certain inhibitors are produced to ensure that we do not act on sensory stimuli experienced in the dream. The brain prevents us from moving physically when asleep.[5] It is possible to become aware of this sleep paralysis in the semi-wakeful state before it wears off. I can vouch that it is quite alarming if you do not understand what is happening! The same is applicable to the experience of trying to call out in a dream but being unable to. Initial research findings indicated that dreams were confined to REM sleep; however, David Foulkes threw considerable doubt on this in 1960. NREM awakenings of his patients produced reports of mental activity in 20–60 per cent of experimental trials. Nevertheless, there is a qualitative difference. NREM reports are less 'dream-like' and more like ordinary everyday thoughts, rather banal and repetitive in content. It is rare for NREM thoughts to be associated with the sensory dramas typical of REM experiences.[6]

It has been demonstrated that people deprived of REM sleep tend to become irritable and tired, and suffer from memory loss and poor concentration. The body tries to compensate for this in subsequent sleep by having longer phases of REM sleep, but where the person continues to be deprived of this, it has been known for the REM state to force itself into consciousness.[7] In other words, after a prolonged absence of REM sleep we would start to hallucinate and cease to be able to function normally. Whether we are aware of them or not, our dreams enable our normative waking state.

We have established the physical existence and necessity of dreams but what about their purpose? The physical need is indicative of our psychological need to dream. In the words of Anthony Stevens:

> We have reached a point in the history of oneirology (the study of dreams) where it is simply not good enough to discuss dreams as if they were purely psychological or entirely neurophysiological phenomena. Clearly they are both . . . Dreams are psychobiological events.[8]

Hamlet contemplated death as an escape from the horrors of existence. Yet he was afraid of the sleep of death because of the threat of dreams. Living was bad enough! What nightmares might prevail after the grave? Dreams may, at times, be frightening but they arise to heal, not to harm us. Dreams occur for our ultimate good and psychological well-being. If they present us with images that we find disturbing, they do so because we need to face the issues raised. Better to awake in a cold sweat than to remain in blissful ignorance of our own destructive behaviour patterns. Dreams 'do not only uncover forgotten memories and present difficulties, but appear, especially in the case of individuation dreams, to have a goal in view'.[9] We encounter our splintered Selves, but the imperative of the dream is always towards integration and wholeness. As we have already stated, dreams are a communication from ourselves to ourselves: that is, from our unconscious Selves to our conscious Selves. We seldom recognize the power and the wisdom of the unconscious. Many of us have had the rather alarming experience, when driving, of suddenly realizing that we do not remember the last few minutes of the journey. Consciously, we do not recall getting from one point to another, but our unconscious Self has been in the driving seat and has carried on navigating and obeying the Highway Code! Many of the other skills that we might learn, for instance touch-typing, become an unconscious process. It is often at the times that our minds are free-floating that we can be the most creative and have our moments of inspiration.

It was Sigmund Freud who came to appreciate that the unconscious constituted the 'very foundation of the psyche'. He saw the interpretation of dreams as 'the royal road to a knowledge of the unconscious activities of the mind'.[10] Anthony Stevens notes that the unconscious was not something that was 'discovered' by Freud but a hypothesis that emerged erratically between the seventeenth and nineteenth centuries. The physicist G. C. Lichtenberg (1742–99) was the first to make a link between unconscious activity and dreaming.[11] The dream theories of Freud and Jung were anticipated by Gotthilf Heinrich von Schubert (1780–1860). He maintained that dream language is 'hieroglyphic' and manages to pack many meanings into one image. Schubert argued that dreams draw on a universal language of symbols which is common to peoples throughout the world, past and present, a clear forerunner of Jung's archetypal symbols arising from the collective unconscious. Carl Gustav Carus (1789–1869) perhaps had most influence on Jung's thinking. He defined psychology as 'the science of the soul's development from the unconscious to the conscious state' and described the unconscious as indefatigable and as possessing its own innate wisdom. He proposed that it was through the unconscious that we remain in communication with the rest of the world and that the unconscious exercised a compensatory function in relation to consciousness – a notion that Jung later developed.[12]

Jung saw dreams as natural and spontaneous products of the psyche that call for our attention and should be taken seriously. On the whole, the dream content relates to the thoughts and events of the preceding day or days. The unconscious is relative to consciousness. Therefore, it is important to be aware of the conscious disposition of the dreamer.[13] However, it is a relationship of opposites. According to Jung, the meaning of most dreams is not in accord with the tendencies of the conscious mind and we must assume that the unconscious has an independent function – 'the autonomy of the unconscious'.[14] Dreams compensate for what is lacking in waking life, warning of needs as well as expressing the desires of the sleeper. 'As a rule, the unconscious content contrasts strikingly with the conscious material, particularly when the conscious attitude tends too exclusively in a direction that would threaten the vital needs of the individual'.[15] For example, the person with too high an opinion of him- or herself may be brought low and the one with low self-esteem may be bolstered up. However, just occasionally, the reverse occurs to exaggerate the point: the arrogant person is raised to an absurd position of importance, while the mouse-like individual is humiliated even further.[16] Dreams highlight issues that we are not consciously aware of, but that we need to recognize for our own good. They function as a necessary psychological adjustment for a balanced life.

Jung believed that not only are dreams compensatory on a personal level, but the individual dreamer may compensate on behalf of wider human history because the individual represents the whole. In this respect, religious compensations play a great role in dreams because of the prevailing materialism of our times.[17] At the same time, Jung concedes that the opposition of the dream to waking life may not always be so clearly marked, sometimes deviating only a little from the conscious attitude and occasionally even coinciding with consciousness. It all depends upon how one-sided and in need of correction the conscious attitude is.[18] Despite his assertion of the compensatory nature of dreams, Jung also proceeds to draw a distinction between the *compensatory* and the *prospective* function of dreams, which anticipates future events. This is not to be understood in a prophetic sense; rather, 'the prospective function of dreams is sometimes greatly superior to the combinations we can consciously foresee'.[19] If we remember that our conscious Selves are only the tip of the iceberg, then it is plausible that our unconscious Selves have more information to go on for speculating about future possibilities.

When the conscious attitude is adequate, Jung gives the conscious and the unconscious equal importance. In such circumstances, ordinarily, the meaning of the dream is to be confined to its compensatory function. However, when the conscious attitude is defective, the unconscious would be given the higher value.[20] This means that the compensatory function of the unconscious evolves into a 'guiding, prospective function', steering the conscious Self in a more worthy direction than it was previously heading.[21] We may be inclined always to associate 'prospective' with progress, but there are individuals who have ideas above their station or in Jung's words 'climb above their natural level', not having the inner maturity for their outward eminence. He cites the megalomania of King Nebuchadnezzar (examined in the next chapter) as one extreme example of this. In such cases, the unconscious has a '*negatively compensating*, or *reductive*, function'.[22] Such dreams are *retrospective* rather than prospective because they stem from the dreamer's long-buried past.[23]

Jung identified one other type of dream that cannot be called compensatory. A *reaction dream* is a reproduction of a traumatic experience. The content of the trauma gains autonomy in the psyche and continues working itself out until the traumatic stimulus has been exhausted. In this instance, conscious 'realization' makes no difference and the reactive reproduction is left undisturbed by dream-analysis. If the dream is merely reproducing a traumatic situation symbolically, as in a normal dream, the recurrent dream will cease once a correct interpretation is made.[24]

Clearly, the psychological significance of dreams is wide-ranging, but I would wish to add a third dimension: that dreams are also *spiritual* events, as intimated in Chapter 1. Jung identified religious instinct with the innate human need to worship and experience the sacred. Dreams allow people to engage with their whole being, and at root is the need to re-own the sacred. Our ancestors attempted to express the inexpressible and pay homage to the author of the universe by means of symbol and ritual. As symbolic creations, dreams are a part of the mystery of ourselves and they are a way in which we are in communication with that ultimate mystery outside of ourselves. Stevens claims that dreams that are 'transparent to transcendence' bring understanding

> that we are moved by energies that we do not control. That is a religious understanding. Such energies are experienced as 'divine' because they come from the biological ground of all being: we do not create them, they create us.[25]

The unconscious lies beyond the physical world in the spiritual realm. Just as we have contact with the physical world through our senses, we can get in touch with the non-physical world through quietness, intuition, meditation, religious experiences and dreams.[26] Morton Kelsey writes that there are two basic forces that oppose each other in the non-physical world: the force of darkness, termed the 'death wish' by Freud, and the life force or *eros*. The ego is caught in a conflict between the two.[27] Jung believed that the psyche, also called the 'soul', is as open to spiritual reality as it is to physical reality, both good and evil.[28] Since the dawn of time, in cultures throughout the world, there has been belief in this 'Other' reality. Dreams awaken us to this reality. Moreover, the more sustained our work with our dreams becomes, the greater the tendency to develop a degree of mystical awareness as the dreams become more mythic and profound.[29]

Our need to dream is, therefore, physical, psychological and spiritual. These dimensions of our lives are not separate entities but impinge upon each other. We are a psychosomatic unity with a capacity for relationship with the divine. Picture a Venn diagram of three overlapping and intersecting circles – the physical, psychological and spiritual aspects of ourselves – our whole Self is the section in the middle. Dreams relate to our whole being, conscious and unconscious, in all its dimensions. However, not everyone attends to the richness and resourcefulness of this inner world. It appears that many in Western secular society are content to live their external lives without ever really noticing their depths. They presume that the external world is all there is. Stevens observes that many people 'treat their dreams like a television set, left on, unattended, in the corner of a room, so that the programme conveys little to them except at an unconscious level'.[30] Dreams offer frequent viewing of an inner world of psychological and spiritual wisdom, giving direction and purpose to life. We do not even need to pay for a licence!

Dreams as a key to unlocking our inner world

It cannot be stressed enough that dreams are highly *subjective*. In other words, dreams primarily deal with the internal world and not the external one. To give an example, if you had a disturbing dream in which someone you knew died, before you rushed around to warn them of their impending death it would be pertinent to ask yourself the question: 'What has this to say about my relationship with that person or concerning the part of me that they represent?' or 'What is it about that relationship or aspect of me that has "died"?' Premonitions are exceedingly rare! Dreams are a message from the dreamer to him- or herself.

> The whole dream-work is essentially subjective, and a dream is a theatre in which the dreamer is himself the scene, the player, the prompter, the producer, the author, the public, and the critic . . . Such an interpretation . . . conceives all the figures in the dream as personified features of the dreamer's own personality.[31]

Thus, interpreted on a purely subjective level, the dream figures represent aspects of the dreamer's personality. However, dreams can occur in which there is a point of reference in the external world. On this objective level, the dream relates to what is going on in the environment; people are taken as real and their relationship to and influence upon the dreamer analysed. Jung provides us with a general criterion to discern whether the dream elements could be interpreted subjectively or objectively. If the person is unimportant or not known to us in reality, the dream should be taken on a subjective level. On the other hand, when the person characterized in the dream is a significant other to us in life, their presence in the dream may be interpreted on an objective level. The dream could be calling attention to our external relationship with that person.[32]

Nonetheless, a certain level of subjectivity remains, in that the guise in which people appear in the dream reveals more about our own perception of them than the reality of who they are. In addition, to make life more interesting, the issue of what aspect of ourselves that person represents may still be relevant. We may need to interpret the dream on a subjective level as well. Often both objective and subjective interpretations are pertinent to the overall meaning of the dream. Just to confuse matters further, we also need to watch out for the dream phenomenon in which a stranger is substituted in a dream for 'someone with whom [the dreamer] is connected by a strong emotion or affect', who may be a painful figure. This depersonalization allows the dreamer to deal with the situation on a subjective level.[33] This often happens in therapy; the client may dream about the therapist in some other guise.

Important dreams may be repeated for emphasis if they have not been heeded. Some dreams have more than personal significance and Jung classed these as 'collective dreams'. Historical and mythological analogies may need to be utilized in order to understand the incomprehensible symbols. Whereas personal dreams arise from the personal unconscious, collective dreams present archetypes from the collective unconscious and have relevance for others as well as the dreamer.[34] An example is Pharaoh's dream about the seven years of famine (Genesis 41). So, let us investigate the different levels of dreaming.

Levels of meaning

Not all dreams are of equal importance . . . Looked at more closely, 'little' dreams are the nightly fragments of fantasy coming from the subjective and personal sphere, and their meaning is limited to the affairs of everyday ... Significant dreams, on the other hand, are often remembered for a lifetime, and not infrequently prove to be the richest jewel in the treasure-house of psychic experience.[35]

Dreams vary in depth and some can be more readily explained than others. It can be helpful to think crudely in terms of three different levels of dreaming. Recall the psychological structure of the Self, outlined in Chapter 1, as you consider the following:

Level 1 draws primarily upon the *pre-conscious mind*. It is that part of consciousness where material has been temporarily suppressed simply because we cannot hold all our information in awareness at the same time. It remains readily accessible to the conscious mind upon demand. Dreams of this kind are usually provoked by our emotional reactions to occurrences in the day past or anticipation of events in the near future. To give an amusing example (that is, amusing in hindsight!), I dreamt the following dream the night before I was due to take a wedding. It was the first wedding of the season and in a church where I rarely conducted services.

> The whole thing is chaotic from the start. The congregation are restless. The bridal party begin to race up the side aisle instead of walking serenely up the centre aisle. I have to steer them around and get them to start again. Once at the lectern, I discover that I have mislaid the hymn numbers and, worse still, I have failed to bring one of the sets of hymn books needed. One of the bridesmaids gets up to do the reading but she mumbles the whole thing and we cannot hear a word of it. Then I notice that a bar has been set up at the back of the church and some of the rather burly-looking male guests are lolling around, swilling pints of beer. I am indignant that they could not wait until the service is over! No one seems to be paying the blindest bit of attention to the proceedings.

This is a classic 'anxiety dream'! I wonder what the bride herself was dreaming before the big day. Before my own wedding, I dreamt that I had arrived without my wedding dress. In a similar vein, before my ordination I dreamt that I turned up without my robes! We could analyse the above dream in great detail and ponder why I dreamt the specific details that I did, but the essence of the dream is clearly evident. The dream images can be taken at face value. There is a rather bizarre turn of events but the elements of the dream correspond to the normal ingredients of a wedding. There are no obscure symbols to be interpreted. It is pretty straightforward. I was worried that something would go wrong – that I would not be in control of the service. The dream has played out a worst-case scenario. It feels as though I am back in role as a teacher coaxing reluctant teenagers on to a task rather than a priest conducting a marriage. Incidentally, the wedding went very smoothly on the day!

Level 2 dreams deal with material from the *personal unconscious*. It is the storage for forgotten memories, repressed traumas, denied emotions and unacknowledged motives and drives. Aspects of this repressed part of our Self emerge as repression weakens during dreams. It happens at a time when we are ready to deal with the issues therein. Dreams at this deeper level employ predominantly symbolic language, which is personal to the dreamer. For example, if you had a dream involving gigantic ants emerging from the woodwork and crawling all over the walls of the room where you were standing, what would your reaction be? Personally, I would be horrified; it would constitute a real nightmare of a dream. The ants would represent something sinister. In fact, my husband had such a scene as part of a longer dream but he was not in the least perturbed. As far as he is concerned, ants are fascinating insects: he is curious about their habitat and how they operate. For him, ants symbolize a community working together with great efficiency. This goes to show how vital it is that we hear the dreamer's own associations with the symbols in the dream.

Level 3 dreams operate at the deepest level, the realm of the *collective unconscious*. This is the level furthest removed from consciousness. Jung coined the term 'collective unconscious' to describe this and distinguish it from the purely personal unconscious of Freudian psychoanalysis. Jung was convinced that the unconscious is influenced by the evolutionary origins of the human species; some universal structures exist in the brain, which underlie all human experience. There are characteristic patterns that pre-exist in the collective psyche of the human race and that repeat themselves eternally in the psyches of individual human beings,[36] particularly in our dreams. Our personal realities are influenced by a deeper archetypal reality, which Jung referred to as 'the two million-year-old Self'.[37]

Therefore, our lives are not determined merely by our personal history but also by the history of humanity as a whole, encoded in the collective unconscious. Jung held it to be the function of dreams to integrate this archaic heritage into the personal life of the dreamer.[38] The collective unconscious is the arena of 'big' or 'master dreams', which can hold great meaning for the course of a person's life and are characteristic of the individuation process. They can often be distinguished from other dreams by their symbolic images, which can be found in the inherited mental history of humankind. Jung writes,

> ... the mythological motifs or mythologems I have designated as archetypes. These are to be understood as specific forms and groups of images which occur not only at all times and in all places but also in individual dreams, fantasies, visions, and delusional ideas. Their frequent appearance in individual case material, as well as their universal distribution, proves that the human psyche is unique and subjective or personal only in part, and for the rest is collective and objective.[39]

Archetypal dreams communicate a sense of great significance to the dreamer, often accompanied by a feeling of dramatic or numinous power. The dream may be set in a historical and cultural context far removed from that of the dreamer, symbolizing that he or she is travelling outside the bounds of waking experience. Such dreams may have a cosmic quality: a sense of temporal or spatial infinity conveyed by dream experiences such as moving at tremendous speed over great distances, flight through space or hovering far above the earth, or may contain astrological or alchemical symbols.[40] Many archetypal dreams involve magical journeys, sea voyages or quests, which often represent a search for some aspect of ourselves and a journey into the unconscious, where the dreamer seeks to find and assimilate fragmented parts of the psyche in order to achieve psychological wholeness.[41]

> Every night we enter a mythic realm, dark, primordial labyrinth, inhabited by the gods and ghosts of our ancestors, and glean from them some of the ancient wisdom of our kind. Such figures commonly take on contemporary guises, but the new myths that our dreams fashion out of them are the old myths of humanity presented in modern dress.[42]

I will now give an illustration of one such modern mythical dream, which occurred while I was training for ordination. You will see how archetypal images have been blended with a story internalized during my own childhood.

Scene 1

I am with my brother outside my parents' previous house – my old family home. There is a huge peach in the front garden. It is reminiscent of Roald Dahl's *James and the Giant Peach* adventure story. Somehow it is suspended so that we can stand underneath it. There is a hole on the underside that I know leads up to the centre but it is still plugged up with peach flesh. Suddenly it dislodges itself, and the whole lot rains down on my brother and me. I am afraid that we will be completely buried.

Scene 2

Now cleaned up, my brother and I are preparing to depart on an adventure in the peach. We are gathering equipment from our cars – pots and pans, etc. I am curious about what is inside the peach.

Scene 3

I am now on a path following four cloaked and hooded figures. I sense that it is another planet. I am unsure as to whether it is actually me walking behind the figures or if I am just an observer. I note that their garments are a mauve-brown colour and not black. Because of this, I know that they are good and not evil. I am content to be tagging along.

Scene 4

Two people (am I one of them?) are flying or semi-hovering over a moon-like surface with craters in it. Every time one of them goes over a crater they are sucked into the hole and then bounce back out again in order to carry on flying. There is a sense of elation and excitement rather than fear.

This was an epic fantasy dream, which will only be touched upon here. It represents both the inner and the outer voyage – they run parallel to each other. It is a tale of adventure and discovery of my Self and new 'worlds'. The initial scene is set at the family home; my brother and I are about to escape on a venture to find fulfilment. My brother, as a close male figure in my life, represents the male aspect (Animus) of myself. Both male and female are in balance. Both the peach and the planet are spherical and contain holes. They are symbols of the Self. Tunnelling into the peach and dipping into the craters of the planet depict the journey into the Self, into the core of my being. Initially the hole that leads to the centre of the peach is blocked but when the time is 'ripe' it loosens out. My fear that we will become buried signifies that self-exploration can be an over-whelming and messy business; however, we do get cleaned up. The cloaked and hooded figures could signify my Shadow Self. The fact that there are four of them is significant as the Self is present in all dreams involving four characters.[43] At that moment they are con-cealed from sight but their identity will be revealed as I penetrate the depths of my psyche. The overall feeling of the dream is very positive.

Jung observes that archetypal dreams occur mostly during the critical phases of life, such as adolescence, midlife and within sight of death. They are also to be expected at other times of upheaval and transition in life, as in the case of the above dream. The dreams mark the process towards individuation and re-birth.

> Since everything living strives for wholeness, the inevitable one-sidedness of our conscious life is continually being corrected and compensated by the universal human being in us, whose goal is the ultimate integration of conscious and unconscious or better, the assimilation of the ego to a wider personality.[44]

These three levels of dreaming are not mutually exclusive categories; any one dream may contain more than one level. You will remem-ber that each of the three scenes in the 'Dark Path' dream, discussed in Chapter 1, progressed to a deeper level. It is helpful to be aware of the general level on which the dream is operating in order to know whether the dream language can be interpreted at face value or, if at a more symbolic level, whether personal associations are of most significance, or whether a more universal meaning is relevant.

The language of dreams

Dreams are poetry; consciousness is prose.[45]

People fail to make sense of dreams because they readily dismiss what-ever does not speak the language of our Western rationalistic mind-set as meaningless. We have become too identified with the logical left hemisphere of the brain to the exclusion of the more intuitive right hemisphere. Ancient cultures were so much more at ease with expressing themselves in myth, symbol and ritual. Technically, the process of dream creation is called oneiropoiesis (from Greek *oneiros*, meaning 'dream', and *poiesis*, meaning 'to create'). *Poiesis* is also the word from which 'poetry' is derived. One major characteristic that poems and dreams have in common is their use of ambiguity in order to create webs of associative meaning to evoke feeling and atmosphere.[46]

Dreams do not express themselves in a logical way but are highly symbolic and employ the basic figures of speech: metaphor, personification, simile and hyperbole (exaggeration in order to make a point). Dream images behave metaphorically when they draw comparisons between two people or things by emphasizing certain characteristics shared between them.[47] This is also a characteristic of primitive languages. What now is expressed by means of abstractions was expressed in ancient literature mostly by similes. We are left with the possibility that the figurative language of dreams is a continued existence from an archaic mode of thought.[48]

The psyche displays a tendency to differentiate the parts from the whole, especially into pairs of opposites, usually conceived as *antinomies* (complementary to one another), e.g. hot and cold, right and left. Linguistics makes a distinction between two primary modes of speech: the *metonymic*, where the words are chained together in a linear sequence in such a way as to form phrases and sentences, and the *metaphoric*, where associations of words are by virtue of shared radical elements (*carn*ation, *carn*-al, *carn*-age, rein-*carn*-ation), by analogy (carnation, flower, violet) and by similarity of sound images. The 'metonymic statements of directed, discursive thought tend to have a single unambiguous meaning while metaphoric statements such as dreams, and the presentational meanings of the arts, are necessarily polyvalent and multiple'.[49] This helps to explain why there is never one 'true' interpretation of a dream.

Dreams are like mini dramas that have a narrative form, with an identifiable structure. Jung was struck by the resemblance between the natural structure of dreams and the formal structure of a Greek tragedy. He identified four common parts that can be applied to the majority of dreams:

1 the STATEMENT OF PLACE and the EXPOSITION set the scene of the action, the people involved, and often the initial situation of the dreamer;
2 the DEVELOPMENT of the plot;
3 the CULMINATION or *peripeteia* in which something decisive happens or something changes completely;

4 the *lysis*, the SOLUTION or RESULT produced by the dreamwork. The last phase shows the final situation, which is at the same time the solution 'sought' by the dreamer. (There are certain dreams in which the fourth phase is lacking and this can present a special problem.)[50]

It remains to see how some dream examples fit into this structure. Clearly, then, dreams are more at home in the world of the arts. To engage with dreams, we would do well to dispense with our rigid linear thinking and enter into the drama of our unconscious Selves. The meaning of the plot need not remain so elusive with some open-minded, lateral thinking. We will encounter various characters in our dreams; *complexes* are located in the personal unconscious and *archetypes* in the collective unconscious.

Complexes are a bridge between the collective psyche and the personal psyche. Jung came to the conclusion that the personal unconscious is composed of complexes, emotionally charged memories, which function as sub-personalities and 'personate' in dreams. These fragments are relatively autonomous and independent of one another.[51] Robert Johnson writes, 'All of us have many distinct personalities coexisting within us at the unconscious level. It is these inner "personalities" that appear to us in our dreams as "persons".'[52] These unconscious personality components lead a life of their own in the psyche, exerting pronounced effects upon our conscious life. Complexes can get out of hand if we do not give them sufficient recognition. They can be responsible for moodiness, embarrassing slips of the tongue and even split personality.[53] It is worth making friends with them!

> Recognizing parts of the Self as personifications of complexes ... making them conscious, and relating to them as one would to real personalities, creates not only greater strength and harmony within, but improves one's capacity to interact with people in the outer world as well.[54]

Where complexes are at work reality can be distorted, perceived through the lenses of the complex. In dreams, the experiences of childhood can be fused with those of adulthood. The past and present are not differentiated from each other. The child's feelings continue as part of the adult's self-understanding, and the ego does not know that it is now experiencing feelings which are no longer appropriate in the present.[55] Pathological complexes are linked with unlived and unactualized archetypal potential which can lead to a life-long quest for paternal or maternal figures perceived as capable of fulfilling the longing that this unused potential invariably creates. For instance, the Mother archetype is the vital nucleus of the individual's growing mother complex. A normal mother complex develops when the personal mother is perceived by the child as having maternal qualities akin to the expectations derived from the maternal archetype, and when she is continually present throughout the formative years of childhood. If neither of these rules is adequately satisfied, the theory is that a pathological mother complex would form.[56]

The idea of archetypes is ancient and relates to Plato's concept of ideal forms: that is, the patterns already existing in the divine mind that determine in what form the material world will come into being.[57] In Greek, the root *arche* means 'first' and *type* means 'imprint' or 'pattern'.[58] Jung noted that 'The term "archetype" occurs as early as Philo Judaeus, with reference to the *Imago Dei* (God-image) in man.'[59] However, Jung was the first to draw awareness to the concept of psychological archetypes. Jung asserted that all the essential psychic characteristics that distinguish us as human beings are with us from birth. He named them first *primordial images* and later *archetypes* – 'Archetypes could be conceived as giving rise to similar thoughts, images, and feelings in people, irrespective of their class, creed, race, geographical location, or historical epoch.'[60] Archetypes are the common 'mythological motifs' that emerge from the collective unconscious and reappear in symbolic form in myths, symbol systems and dreams.[61]

Through studying people's dreams, Jung discovered that the dream symbols sometimes corresponded exactly to images from ancient myths and religious practices that the individuals had no conscious knowledge of. These 'primordial images' had become part of the formation of our basic psychological structure. They therefore arise naturally and spontaneously in dreams.[62] Jung writes that these 'big' dreams

> employ numerous mythological motifs that characterize the life of the hero, of that greater man who is semi-divine by nature. Here we find the dangerous adventures and ordeals such as occur in initiations. We meet dragons, helpful animals, and demons; also the Wise Old Man, the animal-man, the wishing tree, the hidden treasure, the well, the cave, the walled garden . . . all things which in no way touch the banalities of every day. The reason for this is that they have to do with

the realization of a part of the personality which has not yet come into existence but is still in the process of becoming.[63]

For Jung, 'archetypes are charged with their own energy and pro-grammed with their own goals, which they seek to achieve in the psyche'. In this they fulfil the biological objectives of survival, adaptation and growth.[64] The archetypes of the collective unconscious are responsible for guiding the life-cycle of our species through each stage: being born and nurtured, exploring the environment, show-ing wariness of strangers, playing in the peer group, being initiated as an adult member of the community, establishing a place in the social hierarchy, male bonding, dating, marrying, child rearing, participating in religious rituals, social responsibilities of advanced maturity and preparation for death. Ultimately, every individual life is at the same time the eternal life of the species.[65] Our archetypal instincts act as a rudder through the waters of life so that if our core needs are neglected, our dreams will seek to redress the situation.

There are an indefinable number of archetypes. Johnson writes, 'Identifying an archetype is a matter of sensing that one is keyed into a universal human energy system, seeing a powerful symbol that springs from deep within our collective human nature.'[66] The follow-ing seven key archetype dream personalities are highlighted by David Fontana:[67]

The Wise Old Man or Woman, called a *mana* personality by Jung, is a symbol of primal source of growth and vitality, which can heal or destroy. In dreams, this archetype may appear as any authority figure, such as a magician, doctor, priest, teacher or father. Its pres-ence yields a sense that higher states of consciousness are within the dreamer's grasp. Yet the *mana* personality can lead us away from the higher levels as well as towards them.

The Trickster is the archetypal antihero, a psychic amalgam of the animal and the divine. Sometimes seen as an aspect of the Shadow, the Trickster appears in dreams as a clown or buffoon, who while mock-ing himself at the same time mocks the pretensions of the ego and its archetypal projection, the Persona. The Trickster is also a symbol of transformation. He often turns up when the ego is in a dangerous situation of its own making, through vanity, over-arching ambition or misjudgement.

The Persona is the mask we adopt in order to present ourselves to the outside world. It becomes dangerous if we identify with it too closely, mistaking it for the real Self. It can then appear in our dreams as a scarecrow, tramp or some other form of social ostracization. To be naked in dreams may represent the loss of the Persona.

The Shadow, as defined by Jung, is the primitive, instinctive side of ourselves – 'the thing a person has no wish to be'. The more we repress it, the greater the chance of it bursting forth when we are unaware. In dreams, the Shadow usually appears as a person of the same sex, often in a threatening role, or as a stranger who confronts us with the things we prefer not to know. Its appearance indicates a need for a more conscious awareness of its existence and effort in coming to terms with its dark energies. We must learn to accept and integrate it.

The Divine Child is the archetype of the regenerative force that leads us towards individuation. It is the symbol of the true Self, of the totality of our being. In dreams, the Divine Child usually appears as a baby or infant. It is both innocent and vulnerable, yet at the same time inviolate and possessing vast transforming power. Contact with the child can strip us of the sense of personal aggrandizement and reveal to us how far we have strayed from what we once were and aspired to be.

The Anima and Animus – Jung was convinced that we each carry within us the whole of human potential, male and female. The Anima represents the 'feminine' qualities of moods, reactions and impulses in man, and the Animus the 'masculine' qualities of commitments, beliefs and inspirations in woman. The Anima and Animus serve as soul guides to the vast areas of our unacknowledged inner potential. Mythology represents the Anima as maiden goddesses or women of great beauty and the Animus as noble gods or heroes. If the Anima or Animus appear in dreams in these exalted forms, it typically means we need to integrate the male and female within us. If ignored, these archetypes tend to be projected outward into a search for an idealized lover. If we allow them to take possession of our unconscious lives, men can become over-emotional, while women may show ruthlessness and obstinacy.

The Great Mother is derived not only from our personal experiences of childhood, but also from the archetype of all that cherishes and fosters growth and fertility on the one hand, and that dominates, devours, seduces and possesses on the other. The energy of the Great Mother divine is ethereal, virginal, generated from the earth and agricultural. She was worshipped as the bringer of harvests. The Great Mother is an archetype of feminine mystery and power who appears in many forms: at her most exalted as the queen of heaven, at her most consuming as the Sumerian goddess Lilith, the gorgon Medusa or the witches in folktale.

These archetypes are by no means exhaustive. Jungians stress that we should never identify solely with an individual archetype because each is only a part of the complete Self. Individuation is achieved by integrating the many archetypes of the collective unconscious.[68]

> Strictly speaking, the archetypes are not forces, but rather the pre-existing patterns that give typical shape to the forces in us. Nevertheless, when we encounter the images of the archetypes we always feel the power that has been shaped by the image. We feel that we have tapped into not only a symbolic type but also a huge reservoir of superhuman power in the collective human unconscious . . . It feels as though it were something outside us.[69]

Conclusion

Step into the dreamworld and find yourself in some fifth dimension, the immaterial realm, where heaven and earth meet, a 'thin place'. Yet it is no escapist hideout from the material world, for in the dreamworld we are confronted with the very reality of ourselves. That is the function of dreaming. We have begun to trace the contours of this other world, and in subsequent chapters we will explore it more pragmatically. In the next chapter the biblical perspective will be considered. So tread carefully with your dreams and continue on the great quest.

3

The biblical precedent

For God speaks in one way,
and in two, though people do not perceive it.
In a dream, in a vision of the night,
when deep sleep falls on mortals,
while they slumber on their beds,
then he opens their ears,
and terrifies them with warnings,
that he may turn them aside from their deeds,
and keep them from pride,

God indeed does all these things,
twice, three times, with mortals,
to bring back their souls from the Pit,
so that they may see the light of life.

(Job 33.14–17, 29–30)

Introduction

Many uphold the Bible as an authoritative collection of both human and divinely inspired writings, in many different genres, spanning hundreds of years. Its objective is to make known the Creator God, culminating in the incarnation, death and resurrection of his son Jesus Christ. Foremost, the Bible is regarded by the faith community as a revelation of God ('top down' theology), but it also records the human search for God ('bottom up'). It is a two-way communication between human beings and their Creator. Within this vast expanse of literature, one of the ways in which God is shown to speak with human beings is through their dreams. There appears to be a threefold purpose for this: first, as a corrective to turn people from pride and other evils; second, as a challenge for the dreamer to become fully the person they are intended to be; and third, as a form of prophecy. The Hebrew term for dream, *harlam*, comes from a word meaning 'to make whole or healthy'. The biblical approach is very much in accord with the psycho-spiritual understanding of dreams presented throughout this book, that dreams come in the interests of our wholeness, both individually and communally. Dreams are thoroughly respected and play an important role in the whole biblical narrative. One standard concordance lists 108 references in the Bible for dreams, dreaming and dreamers.[1] It is enough to take notice of!

While the subject of visions remains beyond the remit of this book, for the sake of clarity it is worth noting the distinction between a vision and a dream. The content of a vision is given directly by God and it happens while awake: for example, Ezekiel's visions of God and Peter's roof-top vision of the 'unclean' creatures (Acts 10). A dream comes from the depths of the dreamer and happens during sleep. It is the dual creation of God and the dreamer, employing imagery from the dreamer's psyche and providing an avenue for God, the source of our being, to enter into dialogue with the individual. From a biblical perspective, emphasis is placed upon the function of dreams as a means of guidance from God. In approaching the dreams in the Bible, we can learn from the dream messages to the individual dreamers and draw out principles for how we respond to our own dreams. Before investigating some biblical dream accounts, it is worth addressing scepticism.

Why the Christian suspicion about dreams?

Some Christians are at best dismissive about dreams and at worst regard them as New Age quackery or even something to do with the occult! The reason for this is primarily ignorance about the meaning and purpose of dreams. However, there are also historical grounds for this aversion to dreams, which have led to continuing negative attitudes towards dreams to this day.

Up until the beginning of the fifth century, there was a recognized tradition of dreams and dreamwork in continuity with that of the Old and New Testaments. Christians welcomed dreams with openness, as a means of discovering God's will for their lives.[2] However, theologians then denounced dream observance and it was held in disrepute until the latter part of the twentieth century. Why? It transpires that in producing a Latin translation of the Bible from the Hebrew and Greek manuscripts, Jerome deliberately mistranslated a Hebrew word. The word *anan*, which means 'witchcraft' or 'divination', occurs ten times in various forms throughout the Old

Testament. It is a practice which is strongly prohibited. While translating it correctly on seven occasions, Jerome gave it an entirely different meaning on the other three: 'observing dreams'. Through the stroke of the translator's pen, dreamwork and witchcraft became synonymous.[3] Jerome's Latin Vulgate became the standard translation that most other translations of the Bible were written from until the mid-twentieth century, thus perpetuating the false condemnation of dreamwork.[4]

To give some credence to Jerome, at the time of his writing there had been a shift in the incentive for paying attention to dreams. With its now secure and prominent status in society, the Christian Church had different concerns from its early days of persecution. People were interested in their dreams as far as they predicted good fortune and how to come about it. This self-centred attitude was a far cry from the God-focused dreamwork of the early Church, meriting spiritual growth. Ironically, in popular use, dreamwork had actually become a form of divination, and not only for misguided Christians: it also became the domain of mediums and witches. Jerome was rightly condemning the superstitious practice of his day. But it was only in the Western Church that dreams received a bad press; in the Greek-speaking East, the original dream tradition handed down from the early Church Fathers was perpetuated.[5] It is time, then, that we got back to the basics and rediscovered our dreamwork heritage. What does the Bible really say about dreams and how we should employ them?

Jacob's dream at Bethel

Jacob left Beer-sheba and went toward Haran. He came to a certain place and stayed there for the night, because the sun had set. Taking one of the stones of the place, he put it under his head and lay down in that place. And he dreamed that there was a ladder set up on the earth, the top of it reaching to heaven; and the angels of God were ascending and descending on it. And the LORD stood beside him and said, 'I am the LORD, the God of Abraham your father and the God of Isaac; the land on which you lie I will give to you and to your offspring; and your offspring shall be like the dust of the earth, and you shall spread abroad to the west and to the east and to the north and to the south; and all the families of the earth shall be blessed in you and in your offspring. Know that I am with you and will keep you wherever you go, and will bring you back to this land; for I will not leave you until I have done what I have promised you.' Then Jacob woke from his sleep and said, 'Surely the LORD is in this place – and I did not know it!' And he was afraid, and said, 'How awesome is this place! This is none other than the house of God, and this is the gate of heaven.'

So Jacob rose early in the morning, and he took the stone that he had put under his head and set it up for a pillar and poured oil on the top of it. He called that place Bethel; but the name of the city was Luz at the first. Then Jacob made a vow, saying, 'If God will be with me, and will keep me in this way that I go, and will give me bread to eat and clothing to wear, so that I come again to my father's house in peace, then the LORD shall be my God, and this stone, which I have set up for a pillar, shall be God's house; and of all that you give me I will surely give one-tenth to you.'   (Genesis 28.10–22)

Locating the dream in its context, Jacob is on a life-changing journey. To be precise, he is on the run. As a result of the scheming of his mother Rebekah, Jacob tricked his brother Esau out of his birthright by an elaborate deception and now Esau is out to kill him. Jacob has had to flee from home indefinitely until things calm down. He is headed to work for his Uncle Laban, whom he has never met, in Haran. We can only guess at what would have been going through Jacob's mind as he travelled alone. There would have been plenty of time to process recent events. Perhaps a sense of guilt and regret at what he had done, a sense of anticipation about what lay ahead; maybe mixed emotions. A whole new chapter of his life was beginning, but could he be sure that the God of Abraham and his father Isaac accompanied him and still had his future at heart?

As the sun sets, it is time for Jacob to lay down his head for the night. He decides upon the place where his grandfather Abraham had been before and set up an altar to worship God. It is holy ground. A stone for a pillow is not a very comfortable choice by our standards but not unusual for the day. Overwhelmed with weariness, Jacob sleeps, and as he sleeps, Jacob has a powerful, transforming dream. It was no ordinary dream. It can characteristically be described as a 'big' dream as it takes the long-term view, not only of Jacob's life but of his descendants as well. It is prophetic as it looks ahead into the future. Moreover, it has a numinous quality; Jacob knows that he is in the presence of the divine; it is not only his own inner voice that Jacob hears in the dream, but God within him. Jacob is convinced that God has communicated with him. He is left awestruck by the dream that reassures him of God's blessing and protection.

The dream contains both literal and symbolic material. God's words are clear enough, but what about the ladder with the angels going up and down on it? Jacob does not appear to deal directly with the image; he simply apprehends the meaning of the dream in its entirety. However, the symbol does reveal that God is continually connected to his world. It is brought to fulfilment in Christ, who described his own ministry as the movement of angels ascending and descending upon the Son of Man (John 1.51).[6] The dream picture also describes God himself standing beside Jacob. It is intimate; Jacob knows that God is close. He does not simply hear a disembodied voice. This is the God who comes alongside, the one who made promises to Abraham and Isaac and the one whom they worshipped. Despite Jacob's failings, he still belongs to that family and is a part of the promise. There is hope for a restored future. God's promise to Jacob, a commitment to bring Jacob back home and be with him for the rest of his life, becomes an inner strength that helps him to endure the challenges that lie ahead. Ultimately, he is transformed from being Jacob, the supplanter, to become Israel, 'the one who strives with God' (Genesis 32.28).

Deeply moved by the dream, Jacob needs to acknowledge it concretely. The whole episode takes the form of a renewed covenant, similar to those made with Isaac and Abraham. Jacob responds to God, on the condition that God keeps his promise, by making a vow of commitment to God. The covenant is ratified through Jacob carrying out a ritual in honour of the dream. Jacob creates a sacred place by setting up the stone that was his pillow and anointing it with oil. The site of the dream is dedicated as a holy place, where he would come especially to worship God. He even renames the place 'Bethel', which means 'house of God'. Through a dream, Jacob receives the covenant between God and his chosen people, and as a result he will play his part in bringing about the fulfilment of the promise.

In the years to come, Jacob's son Joseph had great renown as a dream interpreter. As well as his own dreams, he interpreted the dreams of non-Jews, who struggled to identify the meaning of the dream, perhaps because they were not so in tune with God, the source of the dream.

Pharaoh's dreams

Then Pharaoh said to Joseph, 'In my dream I was standing on the banks of the Nile; and seven cows, fat and sleek, came up out of the Nile and fed in the reed grass. Then seven other cows came up after them, poor, very ugly, and thin. Never had I seen such ugly ones in all the land of Egypt. The thin and ugly cows ate up the first seven fat cows, but when they had eaten them no one would have known that they had done so, for they were still as ugly as before. Then I awoke. I fell asleep a second time and I saw in my dream seven ears of grain, full and good, growing on one stalk, and seven ears, withered, thin, and blighted by the east wind, sprouting after them; and the thin ears swallowed up the seven good ears.'

Then Joseph said to Pharaoh, 'Pharaoh's dreams are one and the same; God has revealed to Pharaoh what he is about to do. The seven good cows are seven years, and the seven good ears are seven years; the dreams are one. The seven lean and ugly cows that came up after them are seven years, as are the seven empty ears blighted by the east wind. They are seven years of famine. It is as I told Pharaoh; God has shown to Pharaoh what he is about to do. There will come seven years of great plenty throughout all the land of Egypt. After them there will arise seven years of famine, and all the plenty will be forgotten in the land of Egypt; the famine will consume the land. The plenty will no longer be known in the land because of the famine that will follow, for it will be very grievous. And the doubling of Pharaoh's dream means that the thing is fixed by God, and God will shortly bring it about.'

(Genesis 41.17–24a, 25–32)

Pharaoh recalls two dreams occurring in the same night, which share the same theme and meaning. Pharaoh's story is enhanced in the retelling. Greater emphasis is placed upon the dreadfulness of the thin cows and ears of corn. Often, as we relate dreams, further details come to mind. In this case, it suggests that Pharaoh experienced the dreams as particularly threatening. By hearing Pharaoh recall them in the first person, we get a feel of the psychological impact they had on him. Upon learning of Joseph's previous track record with dreams from his chief cupbearer, Pharaoh summons Joseph to interpret his dream. In ancient times, dreams were thought to be divine communications and their interpretation was considered a science. Joseph is not trained in the techniques of the magicians and wise men unable to interpret Pharaoh's dream (who were most likely being politic and offering Pharaoh favourable interpretations[7]). Rather, he believes that God-given dreams will be interpreted through God-given inspiration. Before Joseph even hears the dream, he makes it clear to Pharaoh that it is not Joseph but God who supplies the meaning of dreams: 'It is not I; God will give Pharaoh a favourable answer' (v. 16).

The dream occurred two years after Joseph had interpreted the dreams of Pharaoh's chief baker and cupbearer in prison. Forgotten by the latter, Joseph continued to languish in prison while Egypt prospered. The dreams draw upon classical Egyptian symbols. The setting of the dream on the banks of the Nile is poignant. The Nile was both the basis and the symbol of Egypt's power and wealth, the 'bread basket' of the nation, famous for its grain and cattle.[8] Cows were more than standard farm animals: they symbolized Egypt, the primordial ocean and Isis[9] (Aset), the fertility goddess credited with sustaining life on earth. In the Egyptian towns of the Nile delta, Isis was worshipped as the Great Goddess herself.[10] Throughout the ancient world, the number 7 was sacred, sometimes symbolizing fate.[11] There were also Egyptian traditions regarding a seven-year agricultural cycle in which famine lasting seven years was to be followed by a time of plenty.[12] The seven thin ears of grain that ate the seven fat ones were 'blighted by the east wind' from the desert, known to dry up vegetation overnight.[13]

Joseph understands the dreams as allegories, a familiar category of Egyptian dreams.[14] The setting of the dream is agricultural and so Joseph pursues the line that the dreams refer to agriculture rather than anything to do with Pharaoh's personal life. Russ Parker writes, 'The imagery of Pharaoh standing on the banks of the Nile suggests a nation's leader inspecting the very source of his nation's sustenance and reminding himself of his source of power and wealth in the land.'[15] It is natural for the cows and ears of grain to symbolize the harvest of the land, given their importance in Egyptian agriculture. The interpretation is prophetic; Joseph predicts a great famine. This fits with Pharaoh's own instincts that his dream threatened disaster. Joseph makes four points: both dreams announce the same thing; the seven cows and seven ears represent seven years; seven years of famine will follow seven years of plenty; the doubling of the dream indicates it is imminent and is certain to be fulfilled.

Joseph picks up on one of Pharaoh's additional comments, that no one would have even known that the thin cows had eaten the fat cows as they were still so emaciated, when he remarks that the previous abundance will not be known in the land because that famine will be so severe. The impending famine, unlike many disasters foretold in the Old Testament, is not God's judgement against the Egyptians. Taking appropriate action in response to the dream will avert disaster. Joseph has the plan. A fifth of all crops should be set aside in the years of plenty and kept in reserve for the years of famine. Pharaoh should appoint someone who is wise and discerning to oversee the operation.

Pharaoh responds positively to Joseph's interpretation and recommendations and gives him the top job. Joseph's sudden elevation from slave to Pharaoh's right-hand man is a success story, showing that true wisdom comes from God – in contrast to the wise men who could not interpret the dreams accurately. There is a strong resemblance between Joseph's story and that of Daniel, another famous Old Testament dream interpreter.

King Nebuchadnezzar's dreams

Following the fall of Judah to the Babylonians in 586 BC, Daniel was deported, along with fellow Hebrews, upon the instructions of King Nebuchadnezzar, into his service in Babylon. The book of Daniel details the king's subsequent troubling dreams, which his 'wise men' – magicians, sorcerers and astrologers – failed to interpret. Then Daniel enters the stage to speak the truth of the matter. In considering the meaning of the dreams, Daniel prays, seeking God in the situation, and affirms God as the dream source. The first striking dream of the multi-metalled man struck by a stone cut out of the rock 'not by human hands' was of more national significance. The second, probably much later in Nebuchadnezzar's reign, of the great tree reduced to a stump, came as a personal warning to the king. It is to this dream that we now turn. Nebuchadnezzar recollects:

> Upon my bed this is what I saw;
>   there was a tree at the centre of the earth, and its height was great.
> The tree grew great and strong, its top reached to heaven,
> and it was visible to the ends of the whole earth.
> Its foliage was beautiful, its fruit abundant,
> and it provided food for all.
> The animals of the field found shade under it,
> the birds of the air nested in its branches,
> and from it all living beings were fed.

I continued looking, in the visions of my head as I lay in bed, and there was a holy watcher, coming down from heaven. He cried aloud and said:

> 'Cut down the tree and chop off its branches,
>   strip off its foliage and scatter its fruit.
> Let the animals flee from beneath it
>   and the birds from its branches.
> But leave its stump and roots in the ground,
>   with a band of iron and bronze,
>   in the tender grass of the field.
> Let him be bathed with the dew of heaven,
>   and let his lot be with the animals of the field
>   in the grass of the earth.
> Let his mind be changed from that of a human,
>   and let the mind of an animal be given to him.
> And let seven times pass over him.
> The sentence is rendered by decree of the watchers,
>   the decision is given by order of the holy ones,
> in order that all who live may know
>   that the Most High is sovereign over the kingdom of mortals;
> he gives it to whom he will
>   and sets over it the lowliest of human beings.'

(Daniel 4.10–17)

King Nebuchadnezzar's rule was that of an authoritarian despot, who boasted of his great achievements. Babylon was a power not to be reckoned with. The myth of the cosmic tree reassured the ancient Near Eastern world that the life and resources of the cosmos were secure;[16] however, the holy watcher decrees otherwise. 'Watchers' were believed to be mighty spiritual beings that watched over the universe. The dream caused the king much unrest. While he desired a favourable interpretation, in the end he was prepared to hear Daniel out despite Daniel's own evident distress upon hearing the dream. Again, the text makes it abundantly clear that it is not Daniel or any other 'wise man' who does the interpreting, 'but there is a God in heaven who reveals mysteries' (2.28). King Nebuchadnezzar himself recognizes that Daniel 'is endowed with a spirit of the holy gods' (4.9), which gives him the wisdom to interpret his dreams.

Daniel interprets the second dream

> The tree that you saw . . . it is you, O king! You have grown great and strong. Your greatness has increased and reaches to heaven, and your sovereignty to the ends of the earth. And whereas the king saw a holy watcher coming down from heaven and saying, 'Cut down the tree and destroy it, but leave its stump and roots in the ground, with a band of iron and bronze, in the grass of the field; and let him be bathed with the dew of heaven, and let his lot be with the animals of the field, until seven times pass over him' – this is the interpretation, O king, and it is a decree of the Most High that has come upon my lord the king: You shall be driven away from human society, and your dwelling shall be with the wild animals. You shall be made to eat grass like oxen, you shall be bathed with the dew of heaven, and seven times shall pass over you, until you have learned that the Most High has sovereignty over the kingdom of mortals, and gives it to whom he will. As it was commanded to leave the stump and roots of the tree, your kingdom shall be re-established for you from the time that you learn that Heaven is sovereign. Therefore, O king, may my counsel be acceptable to you: atone for your sins with righteousness, and your iniquities with mercy to the oppressed, so that your prosperity may be prolonged. (Daniel 4.20–7)

Daniel reflects the dream back to Nebuchadnezzar, as part of the interpretation process. Nebuchadnezzar and his Babylon had become God-like, aspiring to rule and provide for the whole world. But reaching up to heaven suggests a rebellious arrogance on the king's part, which provokes heaven's judgement. Nebuchadnezzar's ambitious pride, his turning against God and his injustice can be tolerated no longer. The great tree has to be felled to show that God rules, proving who is really king. Human authority has to be kept in its place; it is helpless outside of the divine permission. Nebuchadnezzar is promised that he can be king only when he acknowledges that actually he is not, because God is. There is a glimmer of hope in that the tree is not totally destroyed; the stump remains. The tree had provided for the animals, now it is provided for in the midst of them. It is treated like an animal, which turns out to be a human being deprived of its senses. Worse still, the life and resources of the nation were embodied in the person of the king, who sustained its life and destiny.[17] The heaven to which Nebuchadnezzar reached will supply his needs as he supplied those of the rest of creation. His abasement will last for a lengthy unspecified period of time but not for ever. In the end he will need to look to the Lord as the real source of help to whom worship is due, rather than pretending to be self-sufficient. Yet, instead of heeding the challenging dream message, Nebuchadnezzar ignores Daniel's suggested follow-up action to repent and set matters aright. He carries on just as before until a year later, when suddenly, in a boastful moment, the dream prophecy is fulfilled. The king becomes insane and is only healed when he acknowledges God as the supreme ruler. At the end of his years, Nebuchadnezzar is dramatically transformed into the king who glorifies the King of heaven.

Joseph the Carpenter's dreams

Matthew's account of the nativity is rich with dream material. The following passage concerning Joseph's decision to have his marriage contract dissolved quietly, upon learning of his betrothed's pregnancy, will be familiar to many:

> But just when he had resolved to do this, an angel of the Lord appeared to him in a dream and said, 'Joseph, son of David, do not be afraid to take Mary as your wife, for the child conceived in her is from the Holy Spirit. She will bear a son, and you are to name him Jesus, for he will save his people from their sins.' (Matthew 1.20–1)

There is no beating about the bush with this dream – no clever symbolism to toy with, or, at least, not in the way in which it has been recorded. The verbal message is direct and urgent and holds prominence over any visual detail of the scene. Joseph listens to the dream and acts upon it even though it contravenes Jewish custom, which dictates that he should have Mary either stoned to death or sent away from the community.[18] He certainly would not be expected to marry an 'adulterous' woman. By taking her into his home, Joseph is exposing himself to possible public shame as well. Why would he take the risk? Joseph accepts that the dream is from a higher authority than Jewish law or custom. The dream came from God, with an angel as his messenger. On the one hand, it would have been immensely reassuring at a time of turmoil; on the other, it must have added to his confusion: the idea of God being human was blasphemous to Jews. A radical rethink would be required. Joseph is given the grace he needs to act with love and compassion, to ensure the safe arrival and upbringing of the Messiah.

After the birth of Jesus, an angel of the Lord again appeared to Joseph in a dream, warning him of the threat ahead.

> Now after they had left, an angel of the Lord appeared to Joseph in a dream and said, 'Get up, take the child and his mother, and flee to Egypt, and remain there until I tell you; for Herod is about to search for the child, to destroy him.' (Matthew 2.13)

This dream carries an even greater sense of urgency than the last and requires immediate action. As with the previous dream, the message is clear: Joseph responds swiftly and they depart to stay in Egypt. Once Herod had died, Joseph was informed in another dream of the change in situation and instructed to take Mary and Jesus to Israel. However, danger was still lurking as Herod's son Archelaus, a notorious tyrant, was on the throne. Yet another dream directed Joseph to take his family to live in Nazareth in Galilee, governed by another of Herod's sons, Herod Antipas, who was less of a threat (Matthew 2.19–23). Evidently, then, God made use of dreams as a primary mode of communication with Joseph to ensure the well-being of his son. If Joseph had brushed the dreams aside as nonsense, then history would have woven a very different tale.

Matthew records only the essence of the infancy narrative dreams to suit his evangelistic purposes. He is not interested in the dreamwork process. The original content of the dreams may not have been so edited and direct. It is possible that the Gospel writer is simply relaying the meaning of the dreams, after Joseph had grappled with them and come to an understanding of the symbolic material.[19] We will never know.

Conclusion

A number of points can be drawn from this excursion into biblical dream accounts and dreamwork. The understanding that God speaks to people through dreams is well attested. All the dreams related here herald important messages from the Creator. They show how dreams promote not only psychological growth but also meaning and purpose in the spiritual realm. While the dreams often address personality issues, such as the egotism of King Nebuchadnezzar, they also have bigger destiny issues at stake. There are life choices to be made. Whereas, ordinarily, a dream is more of a question than an answer, presenting possibilities rather than a particular route to take, the typical biblical examples given are somewhat more direct and prophetic. Such dreams evoke a sense of awe and wonder and awareness of the presence of God. They are critical dreams, not only concerning the destiny of the individual but also having a bearing upon the life of the community. As with other spiritual gifts, dreams can function for the benefit of the whole community. They enable individuals to find their true relationship with God and with the human community.

The dreams all demand a response; this was initially expressed in a sense of reverence for the dream but was followed by practical action – in other words, by dream tasks to be fulfilled. This is to be done with the help and guidance of the Spirit. As God gives the dream, he also gives the gift of interpretation and the strength to carry it out. Believers are to seek God in all things, not go it alone. That is true wisdom and discernment. God is at work not only in the outer events of salvation history, but also in our inner experience. The Bible testifies that working with our dreams increases human consciousness of God's call upon our lives and helps us to find our purpose and direction in life.

> In the beginning
> God created me.
> I was without form
> and consciousness,
> in the darkness of the deep.
> And the Spirit of God
> was moving over the waters.
> And God said,
> 'Let there be light.'
> And my world
> was bathed in light.
> I became self-aware.
> And it was good.
> I was free to discover
> my uniqueness and potential,
> my Being and humanity.

4

Dream logic

Of all psychic phenomena the dream presents perhaps the largest number of 'irrational factors'. It seems to possess a minimum of that logical coherence and that hierarchy of values shown by the other contents of consciousness, and is therefore less transparent and understandable.[1]

Introduction

Perhaps this chapter would be better re-titled 'Dream *illogic*', as to our Western rational conscious minds, dreams appear to be far from logical. Dreams have an inverse logic of their own. The unconscious mind orders its material in such contrast to the seemingly disciplined pattern that we can impose on our thoughts in waking life.[2] Dreams just do not make sense in terms of normal waking experience and so the dreamer is inclined to dismiss them. Our primitive ancestors were conversant with dreams because they were much more in tune with their instincts. In such cultures, the dreamworld was a living entity, with innate power that commanded respect. The notion that the dreaming was like the experience of the soul after death was widespread; the American Indians saw death itself as walking the path of the dream with no return.[3] The ancient Egyptians believed that in dreams their eyes were opened and the gods spoke to them. They practised dream incubation at the temple of Serapis, the god of dreams, for guidance and healing. Conversely, in the 'civilized' Western world, we have become largely detached from that deeper level of communication within ourselves. As human societies have 'developed', there appears to have been a decline in the incidence and strength of the 'big', archetypal dreams, which have been reduced to 'little' personal dreams.[4] A muscle that is not used grows weaker. However, all is not lost, as these basic instinctive layers of the psyche remain part of the unconscious.[5] We need to learn something that the ancients already knew but what for us is a new language: dream language.

According to Jung, our waking thoughts are not actually as precise as we would like to believe. Our conscious impressions quickly assume an element of unconscious meaning because anything we hear or experience can become subliminal: that is, can pass into the unconscious. This both extends and confuses the conventional meaning.[6] Furthermore, such 'psychic undertones' vary from one person to another as each receives the abstract notion within the context of his or her own individual mind. Any given word will mean something slightly different to each person, coloured by his or her own socio-political, religious and psychological experiences.[7] Every concept in the conscious mind has its own psychic associations, which can alter the 'normal' character of that concept. Hence, the expressions of the unconscious in dreams are most revealing, as they are 'the almost invisible roots of our conscious thoughts'.[8] Dreams highlight certain things for us, with sufficient force, to bring about attitude and behaviour change. They aim to restore our psychological balance.[9]

Symbolic communication

> Dream symbols are the essential message carriers from the instinctive to the rational parts of the human mind, and their interpretation enriches the poverty of consciousness so that it learns to understand again the forgotten language of the instincts.[10]

Dreams speak a *symbolic* language. The dream translates our physical situation, feelings, sensations, thoughts and intuitions into metaphoric images and experiences.[11] Thus, dreams often express themselves by analogy. The images produced in dreams are much more vivid than their waking counterparts. Our conscious thoughts tend to be restrained within the limits of rational statements, stripped of most of their psychic associations and emotional energy.[12] A symbol is an image that is endowed with meaning.[13] For Jung, the more basic and Freudian understanding of a symbol, something that stands for something else, is misleading, for the symbol is itself the best possible expression of its own meaning.[14] Symbols are natural and spontaneous products and that is how they occur in dreams. Therefore, dreams are our main source of knowledge about symbolism.[15] As such, symbols are energized images, living autonomous entities with lives of their own. Yet a symbol only remains alive as long as it is 'pregnant with meaning'; symbols may lose meaning and become dead for a civilization.[16]

Symbolic language informs the way in which we communicate in daily life, through creative writing, visual images, speech and actions. To give a few examples: advertising uses the power of symbol to impress its message on the anticipated audience – remember all those bizarre Guinness adverts? Even a seemingly innocent drink like coffee has become symbolic of seduction after certain Nescafé commercials. How often do we use the symbolic love languages of 'presents' and 'actions' to convey to loved ones that we care about them? Then there are those more enduring symbols, shared by society. Leading up to Armistice Day and Remembrance Sunday, people wear poppies as a reminder of those who served and died in the First and Second World Wars. Poppies grew in the fields of Flanders where the victims of the First World War lay. The red colour reminds us of the blood they shed.

The Bible makes use of symbolic language, such as in the creation myths and Jesus' parables, to communicate truths about God and how we should live our lives. Walk around any traditional parish church and you may find a host of symbolic images: the cross; the fish (a Greek acrostic for 'Jesus Christ, Son of God, Saviour'); the dove (the Holy Spirit); the eagle (St John); A Ω (alpha and omega, the first and last letters in the Greek alphabet, meaning Jesus Christ is the first and the last); XP (Greek letters *chi* and *rho*, the first two letters of 'Christ'); vessels and vestments for celebrating the Eucharist. Other faiths have their own special symbols too. Jung writes that these images 'are created out of the primal stuff of revelation and reflect the ever-unique experience of divinity'.[17] All in all, when we scratch beneath the surface of religious and secular society, we discover that every culture has its own vast reservoir of symbols, both living and dead.

The problem is that secular society has largely lost contact with religious symbolism, to its own impoverishment. Jung laments that we have squandered the symbols of our Christian heritage.[18] When the 'gods' are no longer consciously apprehended, they are rediscovered in the unconscious as archetypes: 'Since the stars have fallen from heaven and our highest symbols have paled, a secret life holds sway he unconscious.'[19] That is why it is so crucial to pay attention to ms; they come from not only our psychological but also our spir-depths. Jung expresses it thus, 'Symbols are spirit from above.'[20] the words of Anthony Stevens, 'The symbol is the flesh in which the archetypal skeleton incarnates itself.[21] All symbols are a creation of the collective and the individual. Even on the archetypal level, symbols take on a form that fits the circumstances of the individual, despite being based on a common structure. Symbols can be immensely powerful and impress things upon us, where a literal statement would lose effect. They contain an energy or numinosity, which evokes a response in us.[22] According to Jung,

> a word or an image is symbolic when it implies something more than its obvious and immediate meaning. It has a wider 'unconscious' aspect that is never precisely defined or fully explained.[23]

Whereas a sign can have only one meaning, a symbol can have many meanings. So too, do the dreams they appear in have more than one level of significance. Continued reflection on the dream will disclose multiple, interlocking levels.[24] Although the dream does not set out to *conceal* but rather to *reveal* truths about ourselves, Jung himself was convinced that there is no definitive or clear-cut interpretation to any dream.[25] Additionally, we need to watch out for those dreams in which *displacement* takes place. When a dream is drawing attention to our relationship with an external person in our lives, that person may not be represented directly but shifted on to other people, or even elevated on to the archetypal level. As a general rule, the further something is removed from consciousness, the more it may appear as other figures in order to protect consciousness from painful memories and overwhelming emotions.[26] Dreams will habitually contain images from the memory residue of the last day or so. However, the event(s) will have been selected for a particular reason, and we need to ask ourselves the question: 'Why that particular event?' We should not be too readily satisfied with the obvious. Often it will resonate with past experiences and issues in the interior life. The dream will probably have a deeper meaning than the simple conclusion: 'I dreamt X because Y happened yesterday.' It is also worth bearing in mind that dreams of a single night are usually related to one another thematically.[27]

Insight into meaning inherent in the dream always comes with an interior sense of rightness for the dreamer. Only the dreamer can know with certainty what meanings his or her dream may have, and she or he needs to have that confirming sense. Even then, it is only one meaning among many that is being confirmed. Jung advised his pupils: 'Learn as much as you can about symbolism; then forget it when you are analysing a dream.' The dream content and context needs to be explored with the utmost thoroughness.[28] Dream symbols are bound up with the dreamer. When working on our own dreams, it is no good reaching for a dictionary of symbols, looking up the symbol and seizing upon the 'answer'. If only dream interpretation were that simple! A dream directory does not take into account our life context or associations and, as such, should only ever be used to stimulate thought, not as a neatly sewn-up interpretation. For any dream symbol, the dreamer needs to ponder what that particular symbol means to them personally. Where archetypal symbols are involved, a good dictionary[29] may prove useful in the first instance, but there will also be an application of the archetypal symbol that is unique to the dreamer. Thus, a dream with a universal meaning can only be fully understood located in the situation of the dreamer who dreamt it.

Typical motifs

Dream directories attempt to classify dreams into common themes and symbols. However, Jung did not place too much value on dream classification. He acknowledged that 'typical dreams' and dream symbols do exist but preferred to think in terms of 'typical motifs', which also allow for a comparison with the motifs of mythology. At the same time, he was keen to avoid stereotyped interpretation of dream motifs and stressed that motifs must be considered in the context of the dream itself.[30] Some typical dream motifs include falling, flying, climbing stairs or mountains, wearing insufficient clothing in public, losing your teeth, trains, aeroplanes, cars, frightening animals, being in a hurry or lost in a crowd.[31] Losing teeth is a motif common in anxiety dreams. Many of us are prone to anxiety dreams, especially prior to a significant life event. Certain motifs may recur in our dreams and for some people whole dreams may recur, which adds to their significance. Jung offers three reasons for recurring dreams: to rectify a deficiency in the dreamer's attitude to life, as a result of a traumatic event; or to anticipate a future important event.[32]

So, it is time we explored some key dreams and symbols, under the headings of some typical motifs. Remember that everything in a dream has meaning: the setting, the scenery, the characters, objects and the emotional tone of the dream. All the dream elements provide clues as to the dream message. Not only that but, as Fritz Perls
the Gestalt School of dreamwork made manifest, every little detail

also represents some aspect of the dreamer.[33] Johnson points out that use of place in a dream is usually to show whose 'turf' we are on; asking who it belongs to will reveal whose influence we are under. For instance, to find yourself in your maternal great-grandmother's house will mean you are in the sphere of influence of the Great Mother.[34] To buildings, we turn first.

Buildings

Jung had the following fascinating dream, which led him to the concept of the collective unconscious.

> I was in a house I did not know, which had two storeys. It was 'my house'. I found myself in the upper storey, where there was a kind of salon furnished with fine old pieces in rococo style. On the walls hung a number of precious old paintings ... Descending the stairs, I reached the ground floor. There everything was much older, and I realized that this part of the house must date from about the fifteenth or sixteenth century. The furnishings were medieval; the floors were of red brick. Everywhere it was rather dark ... I came upon a heavy door, and opened it. Beyond it, I discovered a stone stairway that led down in the cellar. Descending again, I found myself in a beautifully vaulted room which looked exceedingly ancient. Examining the walls, I discovered layers of brick among the ordinary stone blocks, and chips of brick in the mortar. As soon as I saw this I knew that the walls dated from Roman times ... I looked more closely at the floor. It was on stone slabs, and in one of these I discovered a ring. When I pulled it, the stone slab lifted, and again I saw a stairway of narrow stone steps leading down into the depths. These, too, I descended, and entered a low cave cut into the rock. Thick dust lay on the floor, and in the dust were scattered bones and broken pottery, like remains of a primitive culture. I discovered two human skulls, obviously very old and half disintegrated. Then I awoke.[35]

For Jung, the house represented the psyche. The upper floor was his conscious Self, the ground floor the first level of the unconscious, then the deeper levels were scarcely within reach of consciousness. In the cave, he found the world of the primitive human race, the core of the collective unconscious. In *Man and his Symbols*, Jung provides a more personal interpretation of his dream, which also illustrates how dreams can be taken on more than one level:

> The dream is in fact a short summary of my life, more specifically of the development of my mind. I grew up in a house 200 years old, our furniture consisted mostly of pieces about 300 years old, and

mentally my hitherto greatest spiritual adventure had been to study the philosophies of Kant and Schopenhauer. The great news of the day was the work of Charles Darwin. Shortly before this, I had been living with the still medieval concepts of my parents, for whom the world and men were still presided over by divine omnipotence and providence. This world had become antiquated and obsolete. My Christian faith had become relative through its encounter with Eastern religions and Greek philosophy. It is for this reason that the ground floor was so still, dark, and obviously uninhabited.[36]

Following on from this, it is generally the case that in dreams, buildings are a symbol of our Self: that is, our whole being – our physical, psychological and spiritual Selves. As with Jung's dream, to be in the normal day-to-day living area, usually the ground or first floors, is associated with consciousness and pre-consciousness; to venture down into the basement area infers going into the unconscious, and to ascend into an attic area is to do with higher aspirations and our spiritual Selves. The kind of building that is in the dream will also have significance.

A house

This is the place that we might usually occupy. If it is portrayed as our own home, it probably represents our ego-house, what is consciously known and familiar to us, the walls erected to protect us from the unconscious.[37] However, the dream house serves to draw our attention to what we are keeping out or the hidden depths and breadths of the whole house. I have had a few dreams about discovering a part of a house that I had not realized was there before, such as the following:

> I am looking to buy a property and view a couple of large split-level maisonettes. The properties are deceptive, as they have hidden bedrooms tucked away down corridors, off other rooms or in the attic. They have a total of four bedrooms, impressive for the type of property. I am pleased with their capacity and uniqueness. Then I appear to have settled into one of them but I am not happy with the bedroom I have chosen. It seems to be in the middle of the house and feels too exposed. The walls are painted pale blue. I decide I would much prefer to have the attic room as a bedroom. I begin to contemplate what colour I would like to paint it – a warm tone.

Dreams such as this show us that there are aspects of ourselves yet to be discovered or put into good use, and perhaps they are now being opened up to us. The house is 'deceptive' because upon an outside, cursory inspection viewers are not aware of the extra rooms. As an introvert, so it is with me – at an initial meeting, people are not aware of my hidden depths. My introversion may also account for why I felt too exposed in the middle of the house; I like to be tucked away. I was most at home in the attic room – that spiritual, 'higher Self'. The fact that it still remains to be painted highlights the creative potential of that room. However, the property being a 'split-level' maisonette could indicate a splitting between my spiritual and worldly Self and the need to be more integrated.

Not only the level in the house, but also the rooms where the action takes place in a dream, all cast light upon a dream's meaning. It is helpful to consider: 'What is the particular function of this room in my dream and what does it represent to me?' For instance, we might describe some of the typical rooms in a house as follows:

Living room or lounge: a place to relax and put your feet up or to socialize and meet friends.

Kitchen: a place of nourishment, where food is prepared, raw materials are transformed. It may be social.

Bedroom: private space, rest and intimacy.

Bathroom: cleanliness, privacy. (If it includes a toilet, it will have different connotations depending on what is happening in the dream and how the dreamer is feeling about it!)

Study or library: work and creativity; the arena of ideas and inspiration.

Everyone will have their particular associations with the different rooms in a house, to do with their own upbringing and lifestyle. When we find ourselves in a particular room in a dream, we inhabit that particular aspect of our own psychic space. Thus, if we are in the kitchen we need to ask ourselves: 'What is the kitchen bit of me?' An unfinished house or a house in a poor state of repair may indicate that work is required on some aspect of the Self, be it the physical, psychological or spiritual condition of the dreamer.

A school or college

This is a place of learning and change. I often dream of being in a school or college building at times when I feel in transition and unsettled. The meaning will, of course, also depend upon one's experience of school, whether it was a positive or negative experience. For those of us who are or have been teachers, there will also be a whole network of associations to do with that role. Sometimes I dream of being a pupil and at other times I am the teacher. There are occasions when my role is ambiguous, as in the following dream:

> I am sitting in a school classroom next to my friend *N*. The desks are in a formal arrangement, in pairs, facing the front. It is the beginning of the academic year. I appear to be both teacher and pupil at the same time. I am sitting in a lesson at a pupil's desk, getting on with some work, but I know that this is also my classroom base as a teacher. (It reminds me of the main block of the school in which I used to teach.) Someone makes a comment about the wall displays not being up yet. I respond that I have not had any display work in from pupils yet as the term has only just begun, but that I could put some posters up in the meantime. I wonder if I can use this room entirely for RE display work; it is the RE room, after all. My mentor teacher from my teaching practice is in the classroom. (Is she in charge of the lesson?) I go and ask her about the ruling with displays. Then a group of pupils come into the room with a big display and start mounting it on one of the wall display boards. I go over to see whether the display is RE-related. It is all about God, so I let them proceed.

This dream occurred at a time when I was thinking about moving on in ministry from my curacy to my first post of responsibility, yet not knowing where I would end up. The procedure ahead felt quite daunting, hence the connection with my mentor in the school where I did my teaching practice. It locates the dream in a time of transition and change, in which I was being trained for my future role as a teacher. This resonates with the stage I am at in life, again being prepared for my future position. The duality of being both pupil and teacher is interesting; that is how I see life. Even as I teach others I still go on learning; it is a life-long task. The friend I am with was put down by certain teachers and never reached her full potential at school as a result. However, some years later she achieved a Master's degree with distinction and went on successfully to complete a research degree. She represents the aspect of myself that can lack confidence in my own capabilities, yet the gifting is there. This is emphasized by the blank walls waiting to be filled with wall displays. A new job is a clean slate on which one makes one's own mark.

A hotel

This is also a place from which to move on and often represents impermanence. Again, it will depend upon our own associations with hotels. For some of us it is a luxury to stay in a hotel, a special treat and a chance to get away for a hard-earned break, perhaps even a 'naughty weekend'. For others, who travel a lot on business, it may be an isolating, tiresome and impersonal experience, away from family and friends. For some it is actually a place of work, and possibly their home.

A castle

Being inside a castle might suggest security but reminds us that the strength of our psychological defences may be isolating us from others[38] and from our very Selves. Of the process of venturing into the 'basement', the unconscious aspect of ourselves, Anthony Stevens says,

> For some, this can be a hard and painful experience, for the apartment in which they live is not so much an attic as a fortress, a heavily defended citadel, whose commanding officers are called Repression and Denial. Defended from the unconscious as much as from the outside world . . .[39]

To dream of a castle or fortress, then, may require that we deconstruct the psychological defences that we have built up over years in order to be more open to others and ourselves. A dreamer had the following dream:

> I am being held captive in Iraq. We are in a fortress, up on the roof behind the battlements. I have a companion with me but I don't know who he (?) is. There are two other men there already, who our captors let go. They tell them to 'run for your life'. Two other men join us in our prison. As the previous two run off, explosions begin around the city. It is pitch black and we watch the flashes of light. Eventually, I think the following morning – it is now light again – my companion and I are released. As we walk away, I comment that we weren't even given as much as a glass of water. We agree that they weren't very humane.

The captors in the dream could have represented 'Repression and Denial'; they have their reign of terror and then the dreamer is freed from his psychological defences. The different men represent different aspects of the dreamer; the dreamer is freed in stages, perhaps representing that in reality it is a process. With the earlier releases the men have to flee for their lives, but the dreamer's ego Self is permitted to walk away calmly and openly *in the daylight.* The inhumane living conditions, reflected upon by the dreamer on release, show that to live under the stronghold of such psychological defences is to be less than human; in other words, it prevents human flourishing. The dream ends on an encouraging and optimistic note. The fear and darkness of the night has passed, and the new day has dawned in which the dreamer is at liberty to reveal his true Self to the world.

A place of worship

This highlights the dreamer's spiritual Self and state. (Refer to the dream example under 'Fire' on p. 65 and the worked dream example on p. 117.)

Food

Food in dreams is to do with more than feeding our stomachs. It is often associated with sensuality; certain fruits traditionally represented lust! More widely, food has to do with how we are nourishing our lives on all sorts of levels. Fruit can equally refer to 'bearing fruit' either in terms of creativity or in terms of accomplishment. Chocolate or other rich food may suggest self-indulgence or guilt. The dreamer's attitude towards the food is telling. Providing food for others may illustrate our 'feeding' of others. I had the following dream:

> I am standing in a public place with a shopping trolley full of staple foods. There is some sort of crisis situation in which we have had to stock up on provisions. I have mainly bread in the trolley – slices of white bread and bread rolls in clear plastic bags. I take a bag of sliced bread, which is starting to go a bit stale and needs using up first, and share it with others.

In addition to being one of the most basic foods, for me bread is associated with spiritual feeding. Jesus referred to himself as the 'bread of life', and in the Eucharist bread is used to represent Christ's body. The dream highlights that I feed others spiritually. However, some of the bread has become stale. This refers to the part of my spiritual Self that has got 'stale'. Yet I have a whole 'shopping trolley' of resources that I can draw upon, and so I need to use these to find the God of my desiring again.

Someone who sees me for spiritual direction had the following dream:

> I am hungry and what I really fancy is an apple, so I go somewhere (details fuzzy) but there is a counter with someone behind it. On the counter are some apples which look delicious, but above them I notice a sign which reads, 'New variety: Unsociable', so I look at the stall holder and say, 'Is this all you've got? You've got to be kidding! Unsociable apples?' and, distinctly puzzled, I decide I don't want them and leave.
>
> I'm still hungry and next thing I am in a big field where there is a marquee, inside which there is a food stall. A stall selling fruit. Someone is behind the table, so I ask them what they've got. He says, 'We've only got this left, "Unsociable Fruit Selection".' I say, 'You're joking!' but by now I'm really hungry so I ask to see this Unsociable Fruit Selection. It looks shrivelled and vile, but one piece, which resembles a Victoria plum, looks OK, so I pick it up. It feels wrong, all slimy and horrid. It smells horrid, too, so I put it down and say, 'No thanks, I'll leave it.'
>
> I sit at a table, pondering this 'Unsociable Fruit' thing, because I am unsociable, so what does it mean? Does it mean anything? And then Lisa and Mike appear; Lisa has long black hair and is dressed like a hippy and Mike is as usual. I tell them of my Unsociable Fruit problem (Mike disappears) and Lisa tells me that I know what it means.

The apple is a well-known mythological motif, most commonly identified as the 'forbidden fruit' in the Garden of Eden. However, the dreamer rejects the idea of the fruit of the tree of knowledge of good and evil being an apple. She acknowledges that apples are not her favourite fruit. It was the one that resembled a plum that she chose in the end. In the dream, that which looks 'delicious' turns out, in the next scene, to be 'shrivelled' and 'vile'.

Upon reflection, the dreamer wondered whether the dream was revealing to her that her unsociable ways, once so appealing to her, are actually rather 'vile'. The dreamer certainly does not come across as a particularly unsociable person; rather, that is her inner disposition, a defence mechanism against the world. She is being challenged to bear fresh fruit in terms of her relations to other people, through a greater openness and courage to 'try them out'. The essential curiosity and hunger is there, expressed in the dream. The dreamer was left wondering what would have happened if she had eaten the fruit. I appear as a soul guide; however, I have been 'displaced' by a guise that is totally the opposite of my real appearance!

The elements

Water

Water, particularly the sea, is the most common and profound symbol for the unconscious.[40] Jung explains that water is the 'valley spirit' and so, psychologically, 'water means spirit that has become unconscious'.[41]

> Whoever looks into the mirror of the water will see first of all his own face . . . The mirror does not flatter, it faithfully shows whatever looks into it; namely the face we never show to the world because we cover it with the *persona*, the mask of the actor. But the mirror lies behind the mask and shows the true face.[42]

This initial confrontation with oneself is quite a challenge, as it is a meeting with our own Shadow.[43]

To dream of swimming portrays our own venture into the unconscious. How deeply we are submerged in the water may indicate the level to which we are engaging with the unconscious. Whether we are swimming freely or struggling in the water will reveal how testing the process is or will be. It is not uncommon, when one first begins to pay attention to dreams and, therefore, the unconscious, to dream of floodwater, as in this dream:

> I am standing outside my house near the sea. It is grey and bleak; there is no sign of colour at all and the area is flooded. I am talking to an unfamiliar man standing in the road. We are discussing the level of the floodwater and I am confident that it will not go into my house. It is right on the boundary. I go back inside to do some study . . .

There is a certain amount of ambiguity in this dream. Turning to face the sea indicates that the dreamer is ready to confront the unconscious. The unconscious threatens to overwhelm. However, the dreamer does not appear unduly concerned, aware of the 'boundary', a defence to keep the unconscious in check. The dreamer retreats into his ego-house assured that the deep sea of the unconscious will not intrude. He is content to acknowledge its presence just outside for the moment. Generally, we are not presented with things from the unconscious until we are ready to deal with them.

Fire

Fire is a powerful symbol that can represent both sexual energy, 'the flames of passion', and divine presence. God spoke to Moses in the burning bush. The coming of the Holy Spirit appeared as 'tongues of fire' on the day of Pentecost. Fire destroys, but it also cleanses and purifies. The Bible talks about the 'refining fire' of God's love. It can be symbolic of transformation or a new beginning. Some time ago I had the following dream:

Scene 1

I am on a country walk with a friend. We take lots of different twists and turns. We are only allowed to go one way around.

Scene 2

We come across my main parish church, now in a rural setting. However, we notice that it is on fire! There are flames flickering inside the nave. It is not raging yet but I assume that it soon will be. Someone is to blame; something was left inside that caught fire, but it was also accidental. I do not see the flames terribly clearly through the windows, as I don't have my glasses on! Suddenly there are hordes of people clamouring around the building to see what is going on. I take authority and tell everyone to stay away as it is dangerous. I check that the fire brigade has been called. I am shouting at the top of my voice for everyone to come away and walk down the road. I lead the way and they follow. I wonder if I have left my cassock-alb in the vestry and conclude that I have, with my green stole. I feel a compulsion to go and rescue them but realize that I can't as I have told everyone else to stay out of the building. I realize that all the other robes are in there too, so if they get destroyed I won't be the only one without robes on Sunday!

Scene 3

I am staying with my friend in someone else's house. My friend goes out to see a woman (responsible for the fire?). She comes back and reports that the woman was at home but would not answer the door.

The dream is set in the context of my spiritual and life journey; there is no turning back. The church represents my spiritual Self, and the flames, the existence of the Holy Spirit within me. It is a gentle presence, which has the potential to be raging. I am afraid to allow the flames to fill the whole building, that is my whole Self, so I call the 'fire brigade' to quench the flames. Yet, at the same time, there is a part of me that desires this. The unknown woman is the aspect of myself who has lit the fire but stays in hiding! I need to integrate that part of myself. Not being able to see clearly reminds me of St Paul's phrase, 'Now I see through a glass darkly', and could indicate deficient spiritual insight, the fact that I cannot perceive the big picture of God's purposes. The fire symbolizes the refinement and transformation which I must allow to take place within myself, without quenching God's spirit!

Now for a snapshot of the three great taboos: sex, death and religion.

Sex

Freud believed that every dream masked sexual urges – *libido*, the life instinct – and was to be interpreted sexually. At a stretch of the imagination, he managed to read sex into just about every kind of dream symbolism. It was a rather reductionist approach that did not recognize the multi-faceted nature of dreams. Jung, however, perceived the general purpose of dreams to be far more wide-ranging. This was not to deny the sexual implication of some dreams; numerous symbols have sexual overtones. When a dream has a sexual meaning, the imagery will resonate with the dreamer accordingly. For instance, a key in a lock is a typical sexual symbol, but not invariably. In a painting by the fifteenth-century Flemish artist Campin, the door was intended to symbolize hope, the lock to symbolize charity, and the key to symbolize the desire for God.[44] A train entering a tunnel may be interpreted sexually for some, or for others may be about their life journey. Generally, objects that are containers may represent feminine sexuality and objects that are long, pointed and penetrating may signify masculine sexuality. A car is an ambiguous symbol as it can be seen as both feminine (as a container) and masculine (as phallic or thrusting).

The general rule is that a dream about sex will be by suggestion; it will be symbolic, with varying degrees of subtlety. However, when a dream is sexually explicit it may not be about sex at all! Jeremy Taylor explains:

> Dreams containing explicitly sexual and erotic imagery and experience also have an archetypal tendency to be associated with issues

of religious, philosophical, and spiritual concern. Most often overtly erotic imagery contains a level of reference to the desire for direct experience of spiritual reality, the desire to understand directly what's really going on beyond the obvious appearance of life, the desire to commune more directly with the energy of the divine.[45]

Thus, more blatant sexual experience in dreams probably has more to do with spirituality than sexuality, although in actuality both sexuality and spirituality are two sides of the same coin. Both our sexuality and spirituality have their roots in the same thing, namely desire. This has been expressed over the centuries in the writings of the mystics; longing for and encounter with the divine is often described in highly erotic terms, using the metaphor of lover and beloved. The book of the Song of Solomon, for instance, has been taken as the passionate encounter of two lovers and also as a metaphor for God's love relationship with humans. Sometimes it is appropriate to interpret sexual dreams on both levels.

Death

Freud took any notion of death in a dream as the dreamer's 'death wish' towards someone.[46] To witness someone we know die in a dream could indicate feelings of anger and hostility towards that person or, conversely, our fear of losing them. However, that is by no means the full story. According to Taylor, death in dreams is related to growth and transformation of the personality. It is as though the old structure of personality must make way for the new.[47] In the realm of the psyche, energy cannot be destroyed, only transformed from one state to another. When a figure 'dies' in a dream, the unconscious energies, which assumed that particular shape, are released and can constellate again in a new form.[48] When we flee from death in dreams, either by running away from enemies or by barricading the dream house against intruders (as in the opening dream account in Chapter 1), we are often fleeing from inner promptings that it is time to change and grow.[49] Accordingly, such dreams are also Shadow dreams; the figure assailing us represents the Shadow and will persist until acknowledged. Taylor reminds us that 'the Shadow always carries with it the very thing which is lacking from consciousness – the very thing that has been "missing" and is required for the further growth and development'.[50]

Consider the following dream:

> My husband and my father have both died and I am standing
> between the coffins. They are on wooden trestles in a place that feels
> like a chapel of rest. The coffins are sealed. I ask myself the question
> of how on earth do I arrange the funeral services, as I cannot have
> them at the same time.

The dreamer's husband had left her some time previously and she
was shortly to file for divorce. This expresses no death wish (she would
even have taken him back) but the fact that it is her relationship with
her husband that has died. The dream comes to illustrate that she
needs to bury her past and move on. At this stage she is still working out how to do that. The presence of her much loved father in the
same state begs explanation. It transpires that this too signals a
change in their relationship. Following her husband's sudden deser-
tion, the dreamer's father tried to reclaim her and be the strong father
for her again. However, he was now too old and frail and could not
carry out that protective role. Neither did the dreamer want to go
back to being the 'little girl' again. She was aware that she needed to
look after her father rather than the other way around. The dreamer is left with the dilemma of how to let them both go, in terms of
what they once were to her.

Another woman had the following dream at the age of 95. While
we might expect such a dream at that age to foreshadow death, in
this instance evidently it did not herald imminent death, as she
relayed it to me three years later at the age of 98! However, at her
time of life, it is still appropriate, on one level, to relate the dream to
an anticipated physical death.

> I was in a church attending my own funeral service. The church was
> a large one with a wide central aisle and long pews on either side. I
> was sitting on the left side of the church, next to my great-nephew.
> Near the end of the pew in which I was sitting was an archway lead-
> ing into a wide corridor. The corridor was well lighted so there was
> a clear view of the coffin, which stood in the centre of the corridor
> on a slim trestle. I was aware that it was *my* coffin, which would before
> long disappear from view. I whispered to my great-nephew that he
> was to be sure to see that people were given lunch after the service.
> The only ceremony that took place in my dream was an announce-
> ment from the person standing in the pulpit, a few yards in front of
> my pew, that the next hymn would be number 159.

We never did get to the bottom of the significance of the 'number 159'. I am sure it means something! There is a wonderful irony in that there she is, observing her own end, and all she is worried about is that people will be fed after the service! There was no fear in the dream, just a slight apprehension. The dreamer had been feeling rather lonely and insecure in her own life. All her siblings had long since died. She had been planning her own funeral at the time and her nephew was her next of kin. The dream seems to mark her own acceptance of her death, the final rite of passage that will take place, symbolized by the archway leading to a wide corridor. At the same time it also has to do with the change of her circumstances and personality in the present, coming to terms with the loss of her siblings and other losses in her life that come with great age, such as loss of mobility.

Religion

As we have already seen in the previous chapters, every dream has a religious or spiritual dimension to it. God is at work in our inner lives through dreams, nurturing wholeness and our relationship with Godself. However, some dreams have an especial numinous or revelatory feel to them that almost gives them a vision-like quality. They may carry a more immediate and direct message for the dreamer. Such dreams impress greatly upon the dreamer, so that they are not forgotten. The following three examples all contain images of Christ.

One woman recalls a dream with clarity that she had some 15 years previously:

> I was somewhere in space and suddenly I saw Jesus on the cross, in space. It was like he was sort of in front of me but at a slightly oblique angle facing to my left as I looked at him. There were all these colours, it was just incredible, the depth of these colours was like nothing you could ever describe or experience. It was a completely different level of existence and it was just so stunning to see this . . . As I woke up the words in my head were 'Who is this God we worship?' . . . It was very powerful. There was no movement in it but . . . it was very three-dimensional . . . It was the realest thing I have ever seen in my life, ever.

The visionary dream of Christ on the cross left the dreamer in startled amazement. As she reflected upon it further, she described it as 'extremely transcendent and extremely immanent'. The absolute total transcendence of God left her in awe and asking the question, but having the ability to experience this most incredible tangible reality that could ever be experienced made it very immanent as well. There was no sense of death in the dream; everything was beautiful, alive and vibrant. She 'knew it was because of him that all these colours were so bright'. There was a sense of the most important thing that had ever happened having been accomplished in the universe. She felt very alive.

> I had a heightened consciousness. I was really seeing what there was to be seen, really being in the moment, and it was absolutely wonderful. It was like a state of being. This is how it is – this reality is *the* reality . . . There was no sense of there being a past or future, just a sense of 'beingness'. It was fantastic.

This dream is reminiscent of Salvador Dali's famous painting, *Christ of St John of the Cross* (1951), of the crucified Christ suspended above the world. In a cosmic dream, inspired by a drawing by St John of the Cross, Dali saw that the unity of the universe is actually Christ himself, and he heard voices telling him that he must paint this Christ.[51] However, whereas the Christ of Dali and St John of the Cross is surrounded by darkness (with the hopeful breaking dawn of light beneath), in the above dream account the Christ figure on the cross is swathed in colours and has a more marked post-resurrection quality to it.

This next dream was again recalled many years after the experience. The dreamer had found it a huge encouragement at the time.

> I and other members of my church were climbing up a mountain of ice. I noticed a swelling in the ice and I scraped at it and it revealed an old boot. There were some strange words on the boot, which I didn't understand, so I decided to show it to Jesus, who was standing at the top of the mountain. The other climbers then started to mock me and said that Jesus would think me a fool for being interested in an old boot. But the Lord looked straight at them and said, 'What she has found is priceless'. I understood that what he meant was my understanding of the words of the Bible, but the others thought he meant the old boot and they scampered about to try and find the other boot!

The ascent up the mountain signifies the dreamer's life and spiritual journey. The dream is packed with religious imagery. As well as the visible presence of Christ at the top of the mountain, the mountain itself is a symbol of divine presence in the Judaeo-Christian tradition and is associated with spiritual aspiration. (Moses received the Ten Commandments from God on Mount Sinai; it was covered by thick cloud and smoke signifying God's presence (Exodus 19), and Jesus was transfigured on a mountain (Mark 9).) The old boot, which some would regard as useless and to be cast aside, turns out to be the real treasure. The boot contains the words of life: that is, the words of the Bible.

After the difficult birth of her first child, one woman had the following vivid dream, while still undergoing a surgical procedure:

> I dreamt that there was a 3D diamond shape, which revolved in the air above me. Inside I clearly saw an image of Jesus' face, as you would see him in a children's book, aged about 30, pleasant-faced with long dark hair. His face didn't revolve but faced me from the centre of the slowly revolving diamond image. But the thing I remember the most is Jesus' words, 'There is only love.' I felt the profoundness of these words – that there was a message to me strongly stating that love is the force by which I should live in the future. It seemed to make sense of my life and almost give me a standard to live by.

The dream, recounted several years later, had indeed influenced the dreamer's philosophy of life. The diamond shape is one of the abstract figures that express the archetypal Self.[52] It also gives a sense of eternity: 'diamonds are for ever'. An experience with the Self is like an experience with God, typified by the presence of the divine Christ at the centre of the Self. The loving Christ image is also a psychological symbol of wholeness,[53] a wholeness that can only be known through the love of others and Self. All of these dreams had a positive outcome; the dreamers felt strengthened, reassured and uplifted by what they experienced.

Some more on archetypes

You will recall from Chapter 2 that the collective unconscious, that deeper level beneath the personal unconscious, is inborn and universal. Respectively, the collective unconscious is objective as opposed to subjective, and Jung later proposed the term 'objective psyche' as a more fitting name for it.[54] Archetypes, then, are the property of everyone, but they appear in our dreams in different cultural guises. In the following examples, the archetypes mostly appear as active personalities, but it is worth noting that there is another class of archetypes, which Jung termed 'archetypes of transformation'. These are 'situations, places, ways and means', symbols that cannot be exhaustively interpreted because of their manifold meaning. They are also paradoxical.[55]

As the totality of the psyche, the **Self** is the archetype par excellence, the archetype of archetypes. 'The Self is not only the centre, but also the whole circumference which embraces both conscious and unconscious; it is the centre of this totality, just as the ego is the centre of consciousness.'[56] The Self is the integrative, transformative, self-regulating centre of our personality that navigates us towards individuation and self-actualization. It reveals our personal potential and possible choices but it remains the prerogative of the ego to make the choices. Co-operation is required between the ego and the Self to realize the aspirations of the Self.[57] Although the presence of the Self is always implicit in dreams, as all dreams contribute towards the individuation process, the Self occasionally appears in the form of a numinous symbol. It can be experienced as a profound mystery or even the divine.[58]

The Self has characteristic symbols, including the lotus, the royal couple (the conjunction of the polarities of masculine and feminine), and circular or quadranic forms, especially the **Mandala**.[59] The Mandala is an archetypal image meaning 'All is one'. The word 'Mandala' is the Indian Sanskrit term for a circle drawn in religious rituals.[60] There are innumerable variants of the Mandala but they are all based upon the squaring of a circle. They represent 'a kind of central point within the psyche, to which everything is related, by which everything is arranged, and which is itself a source of energy'. Although the centre is represented by an innermost point, it is surrounded by everything that belongs to the Self; the paired opposites that make up the total personality. Thus, this centre point is expressed as the entire Self, conscious, personal unconscious and the collective unconscious.[61]

The **Persona** is 'the archetype of interface between Self and other'.[62] It is the recognizable public face or image that we put on, our exterior Self or 'mask' that we wear. Everyone has a Persona. In one sense, it can be likened to Freud's 'ego' and 'super-ego',[63] where the ego is the conscious Self, attempting to keep thought and behaviour practical and in touch with reality, and the super-ego is a conscious or semi-conscious conscience. The Persona can have a bad press, but without it human society could not function. It is the basic archetype of all human society and culture. As well as individual

Personas, there are collective ones, defined by public civic and religious traditions and official uniforms. Some of us have the role of maintaining these public Personas, which can become inextricably bound up with our own personal Persona. Dreams involving personal appearance, especially clothing and public occasion, are usually to do with Persona issues. A few weeks before my ordination I had the following dream:

> I am walking into a large crowded cathedral to join the procession. It is my ordination day. I am wearing my cassock and surplice but then, to my horror, I realize that I have forgotten to put on my clerical shirt and collar. In a panic, I rush back to the retreat centre where I have been staying and locate the missing items. On my return journey, I get stuck in a lift. It is a huge cage-like contraption and I am on my own. By the time I finally arrive back at the cathedral, properly attired, I am too late; the ceremony is over.

On one level, this is a classic anxiety dream. It is quite confused. There is a real worry about being left out. Everyone else there is prepared, whereas I am left as an outsider. In life, I had never had the opportunity to attend an ordination service until it came to my own, and so there was the issue of not quite knowing what to expect, of not being 'in the know'. On the contrary, the cage may also indicate a fear of being trapped by the role. At the outset, I am wearing my cassock and surplice, the correct ceremonial robes for the occasion; however, my clerical shirt and collar, the symbol of being ordained, are absent. I was grappling with what the momentous step of becoming ordained meant in terms of my identity. I needed to be prepared for this both practically and in terms of my own inner readiness. Generally speaking, the motif of being insufficiently or improperly dressed, or even naked, at a public occasion is related to the fear of exposure, the fear of self-revelation as the mask of the Persona is lifted. How the dreamer feels about her appearance in the dream will indicate how she feels about unveiling the Self. In my 'ordination' dream, I was discontent with the way I was presented. As an introvert, I do not welcome being in the public spotlight and the dream confronts me with that anxiety. In ministry, there is a balance between being oneself and also being identified with the role. The clerical collar, robes and vestments all emphasize the role rather than the person. When I dream of being ill-attired, it draws attention to my discomfort at people seeing the real me beneath the clothing. I am self-conscious.

Problems arise when people think that the Persona is all there is and deny other unconscious energies. Whereas the Persona is what we present to the world, the **Shadow** 'is the archetype of the threshold between conscious self-awareness and the unconscious'.[64] It may provide that first doorway into the world of the unconscious. We have already explored this in depth in Chapter 1. The Shadow is the opposite of the Persona. Taylor writes,

> Just as our physical bodies cast Shadows in sunlight, so our psychological personae create a Shadow – a dark outline in the same shape as the Persona where the light of consciousness does not fall, as a result of our habitual repression.[65]

It could be said that the Shadow is akin to Freud's concept of the 'id', the third element in his construct of the Self: a reservoir of psychic energy, consisting of *libido* (life instinct) and *mortido* (death instinct). You will recall that the Shadow can be identified in dreams as those figures we find most repugnant and/or of which we are afraid. Whether we like it or not, the Shadow is part of ourselves and demands recognition. I had the following Shadow dream:

> I am in a Marks and Spencer's department store. There is a rather 'tarty'-looking woman standing near the door. She is tall, skinny and dark-haired. She is wearing a mini-skirt (and possibly fishnet stockings) but, worst of all, she is wearing a fake clerical collar, made up of strips of white plastic so that it looks studded. I have a good mind to go and tell her that it is against the law to impersonate clergy; however, I don't think I get that far. I feel indignant but also intimidated and insulted by her.

My 'inner prostitute' looks somewhat out of place in 'Marks and Spencer's', a shop I associate with middle-aged respectability. In fact, I rarely shop there myself. In such a context she certainly got my attention, even evoking feelings of hostility in me. To my mind she had a right nerve! I wonder what would have happened if I had struck up a conversation with her. Perhaps there is a call for me to be more provocative and not be afraid to get noticed. I need to befriend this more outrageous aspect of my Self.

Jung writes, 'If the encounter with the Shadow is the "apprentice-piece" in the individual's development, then that with the anima is the "master piece".'[66] Within our dreams, we will find male and female counterparts. The archetype of the sexual complement is termed by Jung as the **Anima** in men and the **Animus** in women.

Jung refers to the Anima (and presumably the corresponding Animus) as the 'soul'.[67] It is the archetype of life itself.[68] It builds a bridge between the ego and the collective unconscious, taking us into the realm of the 'gods', a numinous, magical, taboo world.[69]

For a man, the Anima may feel as other than himself, because it is feminine, and so he will usually project it on to women.[70] Likewise, women may project their Animus on to men. This is done unconsciously, thus the person projecting the Anima or Animus will see it as something outside of him- or herself. This has a very complicating effect on relationships! Since the Anima and Animus are so numinous, they are charged with psychic energy, so that they have an emotional grip on people. The person who carries the projection will greatly attract or repel.[71] In the case of the former it means that people are seen not for what they actually are but for what they are desired to be. This accounts for the phenomenon of 'falling in love'. Sanford writes,

> These projected images are the Invisible Partners in every man–woman relationship, and greatly influence the relationship, for wherever projection occurs the person who carries the projected image is either greatly overvalued or greatly undervalued.[72]

When a man projects a positive Animus on a woman, he sees her as a goddess, and the woman can feel suffocated. On the contrary, when a man projects a negative Anima on a woman he sees her as a witch and blames her for his own bad moods, the disagreeable effects that descend on him from his feminine side.[73] The collective oppression of women in patriarchal societies reflects the collective state of the repression of the archetypal Anima in men.[74] If a woman projects her positive Animus on a man, she is fascinated by him and sees him as a hero, the ultimate man and ideal lover. Such projections are likely to be made on men who use words well and have powerful ideas – as became the case with Hitler![75] However, when it is displaced on a man, the woman then loses her own creativity and ability to reason. When the negative Animus comes into play, the same man, who was once so admired, becomes a demon, seemingly responsible for all of the woman's disappointments and feelings of belittlement.[76]

The Animus can play a very positive role in a woman's individuation process, embodying the driving force for individuation in a woman's psyche. He functions as a guide for the woman through her inner world towards her soul. He leads the way, carrying out tasks that the dreamer must later undertake for herself. In dreams, this can be expressed as a man undertaking a journey in which there is some difficulty or danger to be overcome.[77] Sanford points out that a woman needs to recognize and relate to her Animus just as though he were an 'inner husband', otherwise the Animus is likely to project himself on to outer real men. Any woman who ignores the development of her intellectual and spiritual side will have a frustrated Animus; however, a woman who pursues only masculine goals in the world is in danger of becoming too identified with the Animus. A balanced attitude 'maintains an awareness of herself as a person with a feminine soul who also embodies a masculine principle'.[78]

Another character standing at the boundaries between consciousness and unconsciousness is the **Trickster**. It can be either gender and manifests itself in a figure representing both the self-deception and creative possibility of consciousness.[79] Traditionally despised in the hierarchy of social importance, the Trickster archetype can outwit us all to bring us back to our senses. The alchemical figure of Mercurius, with his fondness for sly jokes and malicious pranks, and his powers as a shape-shifter, half-animal and half-divine, is a classic Trickster figure.[80] One of Jung's clients dreamt of the Trickster in the form of a monkey.[81] In the realm of parapsychology, the tricks played by a 'poltergeist' can be equated with the Trickster.[82] One woman had the following dream:

> I am lying in bed and my daughter comes into the bedroom. Over by the side of the room, there is a dresser. Floating by, or even on top of, the dresser is a man dressed as a policeman. He says, 'Here's the dead boy's parents.' I jump out of bed and ask if something has happened to my son. The figure says, 'Yes, it happened at Duxford air show.' The figure has now changed and is wearing the traditional Harlequin outfit, with the diamond pattern on. I come rushing out of the bedroom with my daughter into the hallway, looking into the living room. Then two more figures dressed as Harlequins come into the living room, carrying a body. I break down into tears with my daughter.

In this dream, the Trickster archetype comes in the guise of a Harlequin, an accessible image to the dreamer. Her son lived in Watford, known for its 'Harlequin' shopping centre! The dreamer was prone to over-anxiety about her son's welfare, worrying unnecessarily when she had not heard from him for any (relatively short!) length of time. The Trickster first appears in disguise as a policeman, a 'super-ego', law-enforcing figure, whom one would be inclined to trust. But the respectable policeman morphs into a Harlequin! The Trickster is the ultimate shape-shifter and is out to trick and deceive. However, by his deception, the Harlequin and subsequently his fellow Harlequins are actually drawing attention to the fact that it is the dreamer who has been deceiving herself. The dream reveals that the super-ego, policeman–parent aspect of the dreamer cannot be taken seriously. The Harlequin has come to mock the concerns of the dreamer as being too far-fetched. The incident in the dream – the death of her son – is not really true and she should stop worrying unduly about his safety!

The **Wise Old Man** is described by Jung as 'the superior master and teacher, the archetype of the spirit, who symbolizes the pre-existent meaning hidden in the chaos of life. He is the father of the soul.'[83] This archetype may also appear in the form of the **Wise Old Woman**. Like the Anima and Animus, they are sexually differentiated forms of a single archetypal energy. Jung also referred to them as '*mana* personalities'. They embody the oldest, wisest and most loving possibilities in ourselves.[84]

Jung suggested that on one level, the **Animal** archetype is symbolic of instinctual 'animal drives', perhaps a physical need for food, rest, exercise or sex. In dreams, horses tend to be about the physical condition of the dreamer, whereas dogs and cats tend to constellate masculine and feminine instinctual sexual energies. Anima becomes Cat and Animus becomes Dog. On another level, the earliest representations of shaman figures are blended with animal forms. The idea is that animal consciousness turns into human consciousness and human consciousness turns back into animal awareness again in shamanic trance. This is still characterized in the trance practice of shamans in non-technological cultures throughout the world. Accordingly, the animal-headed deities of the ancient Egyptians represent the evolution of human consciousness into increasingly more developed and individuated states.[85]

Conclusion

As the student of any new language will be aware, it takes time to master it and build up a vocabulary, but one can get by on the basics. In fact, even a little knowledge can be life-saving. The same is true where dreams are concerned. It has only been possible to scratch the surface of all the possible dream motifs, even the most common ones. However, the hope is that this chapter will have given a feel for how dream symbolism works. We will have the opportunity to examine a few more motifs in the next chapter. The heart of it is to maintain that relationship with our deepest Selves, to be open and eager to learn and be changed.

For after all the efforts of the soul, it cannot by its unaided labours make itself fitted for union with God in love. God must take it himself into his own hands and purify it in the dark fire.[86]

5

The journey of a lifetime

The whole of human life is a drama: we all live out our own particular 'soap'. How is the drama created? Jung's answer . . . by the Self. It
contains the whole programme for life which unfolds in response to
whoever or whatever is present in the environment and it expresses
itself in our behaviour, thoughts, feelings stories, and dreams.[1]

Introduction

Suppose someone told you that there was something that spoke to you
every night, that always presented you with a truth about your own
life and soul, that was tailor-made to your individual needs and particular life-story, and that offered to guide you throughout your lifetime and connect you with a source of wisdom far beyond yourself.
And furthermore, suppose that all of this was absolutely free . . .[2]

Dreams are a well of wisdom, from which to be drawn throughout
our whole life journey. They are part of the mystery within us, which
connects us with our past and uncovers our potential. They reveal
who we are, what is blocking us and how we might move on.
Dreams often call into question the attitudes and choices of the ego
(the conscious, decision-making, part of ourselves). To bring about
wholeness, the ego needs to serve not simply its own purposes, but
those of the Self.[3] Dreams come in the service of the Self, to foster
psychological and spiritual growth. There is a close relationship
between psychological wholeness and spiritual holiness. In fact, to
all intents and purposes, Jung's 'psyche' and the Christian 'soul' can
be taken as one and the same thing.[4] Spiritual sanctification entails
psychological development because spiritual development can be
blocked by personality problems; and, vice versa, certain personality
problems require a spiritual perspective.[5] We have a personal voca-
tion to work towards wholeness for ourselves and for the sake of
others. From a Christian perspective, the goal of life is to become
holy and whole, but this does not happen in an instant; rather, we

are on a journey, and this implies both a goal and a process.[6] God enables this process of our becoming whole, which entails both adding new things to our life and letting go of what is unhealthy for us. Our task is to become conscious both of the new aspects of ourselves to be integrated into our personality and of personality issues that need to be dealt with, attitudes or behaviours that we need to make a choice to change in order to move forward.[7] Awareness is half of the enterprise; acting upon what we have learned is the other.

This chapter investigates the role of dreams in life's progression through the interplay of past, present and future. The scene is set with an excursion into the motif of the journey, depicting our great life journey. Then, the role of dreams in healing the hurts of the past is considered before we move on to look at the function of dreams in shaping the future, through an exploration of the inner child motif, creative dreaming and, cursorily, the phenomenon of pre-cognitive or prospective dreaming. This is all drawn together by the grand finale of 'individuation dreams', which encompass the whole of a person's life journey. So, let the journey begin . . .

The journey motif

To be on a journey in dreams usually symbolizes our life journey, in terms of the archetypal quest for meaning and fulfilment. The mode of transport used will indicate how we are making progress with that journey. A **car** is an everyday vehicle. It represents the ego and the amount of energy available to the ego as it goes about its tasks in life.[8] A car can speed on the motorway towards its destination, take the scenic route, be stuck in a traffic jam or, worse still, break down! Where the dreamer is in relation to the car is important. To be in the driving seat is reassuring as it signals that you are 'in the driving seat' of your life, i.e. in control. On the contrary, to be in a passenger seat suggests that you – that is, the ego – are giving your life over to another figure within you and not taking charge. This could be a recognizable external figure that has been internalized, such as a boss or spouse, or an inner figure with no obvious external frame of reference. In either case, the question needs to be asked: 'What aspect of me does it represent that I am allowing to get out of hand?' Where the figure is known, it may be necessary to look at that life situation – for example, the intimidating boss who leaves you feeling disempowered.

An **aeroplane** goes through the air, which represents the world of the spirit or intellect.[9] Dreams involving flying (especially without any transport!) can be exhilarating and an expression of the dreamer's higher Self. However, it could mean that the dreamer is not sufficiently 'grounded' and care must be taken to avoid a 'crash'. A **boat** or **ship** has a deeper, archetypal significance. It symbolizes what carries us through life, the body or the Self or even a set of beliefs. The early Church was symbolized by a ship because it took the believer across life to a safe shore.[10]

A **bus** is a public means of transport in which we lose our individual influence. It may indicate that we are going with the crowd through life.[11] Even more so, a **train** follows a fixed route. Being on the wrong train or missing a stop may suggest missed opportunities. On the other hand, a **bicycle** is generally positive as it is individual and we power it ourselves. The circular motion of the wheels is characteristic of the individuation process, which moves around a centre with a circular form of progression (refer to the section on the Self in Chapter 4, p. 72).[12] **Walking** and **running** are also affirmative means of travel because we have our feet firmly on the ground, advancing in a natural way at our own pace and in our own strength.[13]

On the eve of one birthday, I had this dream:

> A group of us are walking on fairly level, snow-covered ground in a certain direction. We come to a wire fence, which we must get through – there are some gaps in it. On the other side we arrive at a huge mountain. It is where I have been heading. It has a name (beginning with G?). The mountain is black granite; there is no snow on it. It appears to have writing etched on it in hieroglyphics. I feel as though I am standing on holy ground. It is an awesome experience. I am not really aware of anyone else at this point. I think I am so close that I reach out and touch it.
>
> Then I am getting into a boat, just a simple rowing boat, with three other people, one of whom turns out to be my cousin. I sit with her at the back and the other two are rowing us out to sea. We are the other side of the mountain range now and we look back as we pull away from the shore. I catch a glimpse of the most amazing sunset between the mountains. It is absolutely breath-taking. I ask if someone has a camera and whether the picture will come out. One of the men at the front rowing (my husband?) has and takes a photograph.

Upon waking I felt as though I had emerged from a religious experience, and the sense of the numinous lingered. It was a most moving and spiritual dream, a journey of transformation. I begin on foot, making progress at my own pace, by my own efforts but also in the company of the group. Just as in life, I do not make my journey alone. The snow covering on the ground can be associated with coldness, the aspects of myself that need to be 'thawed out' to reveal my true Self that lies underneath. The wire fence needs to be got through, not around. This represents my psychological 'de-fences', but there are now gaps in them and I can climb through. On the other side the scenery is changed; the snow has gone. In particular, there is no snow on the special mountain. I am totally transfixed by the mountain. In Judaeo-Christian culture, the mountain is traditionally associated with divine presence and the letter 'G' implies that the mountain was called 'God'. It also signifies the spiritual Self and aspirations. The fact that I could not recall the name or read the hieroglyphics adds to the sense of mystery – the mystery of God and of myself. Reaching out to touch the mountain is the climax of the dream, but it does not end there: the journey continues out into uncharted waters. The boat symbolizes what carries me through life, out into the deep sea of the unconscious. I can still look back at the mountain in all its magnificence and see the sun setting on my past as I head out to the future.

Past: Inner healing

> In these times of his Spirit, God wishes again to speak his healing word frequently through dreams (Acts 2.17) so that our lives may be guided by his Spirit rather than by our fear, anxiety, anger and guilt buried in our subconscious.[14]

The popular expression 'time is a great healer' is particularly unhelpful. It really depends on what you do with the time. We are like onions; we conceal layer upon layer of experience. It is not automatic that each emotional hurt we suffer will be healed; rather, it is covered over by layer upon layer of further life experience. The wound is no longer on the surface, for others to see or even to be recognized by ourselves. However, it can be dissected and when it is, the presenting feelings can be surprisingly raw. Dreams get us in touch with those deeper layers of ourselves. They expose memories forgotten in daily consciousness that still affect our inner lives, drives and actions without us even realizing it. These emotionally charged memories make up our 'complexes' (see Chapter 2). Dreams confront us with how complexes are interfering with our lives and then collaborate with our conscious Selves to restructure them, liberating the archetypal potential for growth.[15] Nonetheless, it must be warned that this is not easy work:

> However much we might wish to get free from our complexes . . . *our complexes are us*: they are . . . the armature around which our personal identity is built. To begin dismantling these vital structures can be a threat to the security of one's very existence.[16]

We need to be sensitive to ourselves and to others in this process and not rush things or force change before we are ready. Dreams work by analogy; they recall things from the past that are analogous to an event in the present. The current situation acts as a catalyst to release the past occurrence. Instead of putting new documents in new files, when the mind sees resemblances to the contents of other records filed it collates them with the existing files and improvises upon the original motifs.[17] When there are images from the past in a dream, there will have been an incident in the present that has an emotional correspondence with the past event, highlighting that the past experience has not yet been fully resolved. The unconscious can be either healing or destructive, depending upon how we relate to it. When we do not recognize how the unconscious is affecting us, situations in the present may resonate with negative experiences in the past, triggering inappropriate reactions in the present. Unless we understand where these unhelpful gut reactions come from, we will continue to act out of our psychological defences. On the contrary, when we have a grasp of what is happening within us, this same power of the unconscious is healing and transformative.[18] Dreams, if we pay attention to them, are enormously healing because they carry energy from the unconscious to the conscious.[19] In other words, they can energize us and initiate the momentum for change. For healing to take place requires the conscious to co-operate with the unconscious. 'To come to the unconscious as a supplicant desiring wholeness puts us in the right attitude to find inner healing.'[20]

The paradoxical nature of the unconscious is often symbolized in dreams by the snake or serpent. To be bitten by the serpent shows that we are vulnerable to the unconscious. Its 'bite' can become either a destructive poison, eating away at us, or a medicine that heals us. As such, the serpent, one of the most feared creatures, is a symbol for healing, transformation and eternal life.[21] Once I had a dream containing the following scene:

I am in a jungle-like area. There is a slender snake staring at me with its sharp eyes. Then it bites my finger. I appear to be with another female teacher, who is older than me and seems in control of the situation, and there is also a man there, but no one else. They say that the poison needs to be cut out. I am terrified of this prospect but agree as I know there is no alternative and I trust them. We sit on the grass and the woman takes my hand in order to perform the procedure. The dream ends.

On an archetypal level, the dream illustrates how the inner disorder of my unconscious life was emerging to 'bite' me. Associating the serpent with the mythical serpent in the Garden of Eden, it could be seen as the source of my selfish and poisonous instincts. The other female figure is a form of the Wise Old Woman archetype, again a primal source of energy that can either heal or destroy. She is the aspect of myself who comes to my aid, but not without inflicting suffering; I am the one who has the potential to heal myself. There is a balance of male and female in the dream; the male complement of myself, the Animus, is helping the woman carry out the healing process. The dream occurred at quite a testing time in my life and challenges me to examine the venom within myself that could either poison my life and relationships or bring about healing. The procedure is shown to be rather drastic, incisive and painful, as maybe that is how I was experiencing it. The way to self-understanding and change is not always a comfortable ride.

Disturbing dreams, such as the above or worse, are often referred to as 'nightmares'. They are those dreams in which the dreamer feels helpless in the presence of a danger and is overwhelmed by fear or anxiety. They are powerful enough, sometimes, to wake the dreamer from sleep and continue to trouble him or her throughout the day. The Anglo-Saxon word *mare* meant demon; however, nightmares are usually far from demonic! Instead, their alarming nature attracts attention to potentially threatening situations that the dreamer has failed to confront and provides valuable opportunities for learning and growth.[22] Really, there is no such thing as a 'nightmare' (in terms of a distinct category of dream) as all dreams come in the interest of healing and wholeness. Nightmares are to be tackled in the same way as any other dream.

Dreams can be instrumental for the healing of memories. Take the case of one woman, in her early forties, whose brother had taken his own life at the age of 14. She was only six and a half at the time and her family refused to talk about it. She had struggled with unresolved grief ever since. Then she had an epic dream, recalling her past, that was life-changing for her. It is recounted, in part, below:

I had gone back to W— Street in B— where I'd lived from June 1968 to January 1980.

At first I thought I was driving round the streets, but I was higher, as if in a plane that was flying very low. I wasn't aware of being in a vehicle of any kind, though. I knew that I wasn't in the present time because today the prefabs have all gone and even the street isn't there any more. As we swept down W— Street from the direction of the park end I felt very excited . . . I was delighted to see it all again. We moved quite quickly, it seemed like a matter of seconds, and it was a surprise to be there and my mind was full trying to remember who lived where. I only had time to see curtains and then brief glimpses of people walking across the site, as we turned right into S— Road . . . Then I saw the back of Nan's prefab with the curtains that were orange and green with yellow irises on and moved past into the Greyhound pub, where we landed and went down for a long way in a lift, deep into the earth. That was the way into this world. I came out of this dark pub and then walked to my Nan's place, 150 yards back along the road.

It had been raining a bit, I think. The ground was damp and the sky grey and cloudy, but it was warm. I walked up to my Nan's back door . . . They were pleased to see me as if they already knew me, but I knew that they didn't actually know who I was. I was still excited about making my amazing statement. But I paused and took my time to look round and see who was there. On my immediate right was my mum (the age when she died, 64), then my Nan standing by the kitchen door (about 65 to 70), then we had two more people, then me, sitting next to my cousin Samantha (aged eight), then her mum, my Aunt Loretta (about 60), then the usual furniture, dresser, TV, then Roger (about 60) then my dad (about 60). He was sitting in the chair under the window and looked at me, really pleased to see me. He was the one I was most excited about telling . . . I knew with confidence that this was 1973, maybe because of the way I was dressed in a red dress that my mum had bought me . . . I also knew it was early summer, May time, and I would have been 12. Mum didn't notice my arrival. It was very squashed in there.

I had the thought, 'What will they think of me?' before I announced, 'It's me! I'm Julie, I've come back in time, and I'm from the future!' 'Oh!' they said, as if I was a visitor from China. They weren't at all curious and didn't ask any questions. Just excited I was there.

There was a lot of excited talking going on and I was trying to explain to my dad about going back in time and about the lift; we talked about the process, not about the future or what it was like. I have a vague recollection that I knew we would have to talk about the mechanics of it before we could talk about me. Or was it I knew we'd never talk about me?

Then my other cousin Linda was next to me, saying, 'She's still really hurting, you know.' I didn't know who she was talking about for a minute, and then I realized she was talking about the 12-year-old Julie, and I said in a confiding sort of way, 'Yes, you know, I still am, even after 30 years.' 'Really?!' she exclaimed, surprised, and I thought, 'Yes, actually I am. Not as much, but still hurting.'

Then I remember walking outside and up the road to B— Road. I was having a lovely time and I was so happy, I wanted to stay here. This was my home. It felt warm and inviting and I loved it . . .

I must have made my way to where Bill was buying a newspaper. He was walking towards me, holding the paper out in front of him, reading. There was a counter, painted white, with newspapers spread out on top of it . . . I climbed over the counter, and the next thing I knew I was in Concord House, in the present, back in the future, and the counter with the newspapers had become a kitchen work-surface type counter with newspapers on . . .

I started telling Sister Margo about my dream, and as I did this I realized that the dream was confirming that I should be at Concord House, as the man in the doorway was called Mr Hope and he taught French. It was through talking to him that I came back to the real present. I was ecstatic. I felt that I had been given a big present from God and I had a new confidence in the future that all would be well. Hope – that was the big thing. I was so excited about it, telling Sister Margo, marvelling at the cleverness of it all.

Following the dream the dreamer was awestruck:

I woke up then, full of this same hope. I felt really joyous. What a wonderful dream! First thoughts are: (1) acknowledge the pain of your loss; (2) recognize the pulling to stay in the past and not stay in the present; (3) you have been given the gift of hope; (4) your picture of the past is imperfect.

The merging of past and present in the dream illustrates the timeless nature of the dream reality, that the events of the past can have a huge unconscious hold on the present. In drawing attention to her buried grief, the dream gave the dreamer a sense of release and healing from the negative feelings about her brother that were holding her back. It was an incredibly positive and happy experience, which brought her to a decision point; she had the choice either to remain trapped by the past or to move on and live in the present. She made the conscious decision to live in the present and to deal with the life problems of the present, which she had been avoiding by living in the past. On a subsequent retreat she was able to forgive her brother, which was immensely healing for her. At the same time, the dream also spurs her into the future as it raises for her the issue of current life choices that call for discernment.

Where a dream unveils a specific memory that needs healing, identification of the past hurt is one thing but healing it may be another. Dreams can be very healing in themselves when their message is heeded, but sometimes further work is needed. In the preceding example, the dreamer had to actively forgive her brother for his suicide. In their book *Healing Life's Hurts*, Dennis and Matthew Linn liken the healing of a memory to the grief process. The five stages of denial, anger, bargaining, depression and acceptance become: I don't admit I was ever hurt; I blame others for hurting and destroying me; I set up conditions to be fulfilled before I'm ready to forgive; I blame myself for letting hurt destroy me; I look forward to growth from hurt.[23] The five stages need to be worked through before the hurt can become fully healed. This can be accomplished in prayer by sharing the different feelings experienced at each stage with Christ and listening for his response. The length of the process will depend upon the degree of the hurt; it may be necessary to spend several prayer sessions on just one stage. Attention is drawn to the significance of dreams in uncovering past hurts. One Linn writes, 'I usually go to bed saying, "Jesus . . . Bring to mind a dream that will heal whatever way I cannot yet absorb your love." '[24] The feeling content of a dream is especially helpful here, both generally and in the feelings of the different characters in the dream, representing the different aspects of ourselves. Each can be asked how they are feeling, and then we can ask ourselves when we most felt that way. As well as praying through the five stages above, another way of working with the dream or memory is to imagine Jesus entering either the dream scene or the memory that the dream recalls, and to observe Jesus' reactions (see Chapter 6). Alternatively, the dream and the memory or feelings it stirs up could be talked through with an empathetic listener; a counsellor, spiritual director or trusted friend, in order to further the healing process.

Potential

The inner child motif

As a general rule, the presence of children in our dreams is not primarily concerned with any literal offspring that we may have but is symbolic of those aspects of our own personality, i.e. our own 'inner child'. In her book *The Inner Child in Dreams*, Kathrin Asper explores the significance of the role of the inner child motif as pointing to something new and future-orientated. There are certain points in life when the inner child may become more evident in our dreams – at times of change and transition, midlife and approaching death. Our inner child incorporates the child that we once were (indirectly), our spontaneous, childlike aspects and our creative possibilities.[25]

> The child as symbol mirrors not outer reality but rather the inner reality of the psyche and reflects the wishes, hopes, and longings to which we aspire. Thus the child becomes a symbol of that which is new and yet to come.[26]

An awareness and appreciation of the child we once were is nonetheless integral to this process. Dreams can show the way in which the experiences of childhood are fused with those of adulthood.[27] However, our dreams will rarely directly reveal to us ourselves as a child. We will need to work with the guises that dreams employ. The emotional experience of the child remains with the adult and unconsciously influences the adult's actions and reactions. The problem is that even though as adults we differentiate ourselves from our parents, in certain situations we behave as if we were still children and project an unhelpful parent complex on to other people.[28] This will have a detrimental effect upon the relationships concerned and hinder progress in life in general. It can take a long time to become aware of the origin of these feelings, to recognize them as inappropriate for the present and to change behaviour patterns.

Many of us pay little heed to the child within. By dismissing the inner child, we cut ourselves off from that part of ourselves that needs nurturing. Asper writes, 'The Self as it appears in the figure of the child is often that to which we give little attention.'[29] This can become manifest in the dream content itself. A while ago, to my consternation, the dream motif of the 'mischievous child' began to pop up in my dreams.

Car theft

Scene 1

I am back at the school where I used to teach, supply teaching during my summer holidays. I am coming to the end of my spell there and am telling the head I will be off in a couple of days. She looks a bit sallow and sour.

Scene 2

I am in the car park saying my goodbyes. As I approach my car, to my horror I see three girls and a woman jump in. It is someone I know from church and her daughters. Katie, the youngest and most mischievous one, has taken the driving seat. She is starting up the ignition. I spot the keys and wonder how she has got the spare set. The car lurches away and drives out on to the road. I chase after it, yelling for her to stop, and the car grinds to a halt. I rush over and take the driving seat (with the others still in the car). First of all, I pull over on to the verge for a moment to catch my breath. I feel a bit shaken by the incident. It could have been very dangerous.

Scene 3

I am back at the family's house. I am standing in the living room. An elderly lady (the grandmother?) is there, challenging me about something. We have a conversation. The children are sitting on the floor playing in the hall. I feel obliged to sit down and join in with them briefly before I leave.

The opening locates the dream at the phase of my life when I was training for ministry, as during that time I had the opportunity to do some supply teaching at my previous school in the overlap at the end of the college term. At the same time, there is an awareness of my present life, inferred by the other characters in the dream. The two periods of my life are merged together somehow. My time at theological college may be alluded to because it was there that I acquired a 'spirit of naughtiness' (extra curricular!), lacking in my own childhood. However, since ordination I have had to be 'grown up' again, just as when I was a teacher.

The 'me' in the dream is there in the role of the teacher. It is the super-ego, law-enforcing, part of the Self, emphasized by the presence of the headmistress at the start of the dream. However, this authority figure is dramatically challenged by the actions of 'Katie' and her mother and sisters as accessories to the crime! It is interesting that even her very well-behaved sister, representing the 'good girl' in me, went along with it. Not only does Katie have the audacity to mis-behave, she literally takes over the driving seat of my life! To have my ego Self removed from the wheel feels very dangerous, and so the super-ego aspect of me puts a stop to it!

Katie is cheeky, wilful, playful and amusing! The dream is con-fronting me with the playful child in me, inclined to naughtiness, which has been in Shadow. Despite my fears of what calamity might befall the car and its passengers, the incident is to be interpreted in a creat-ive rather than destructive sense. This is reinforced by the children 'at play' in the final scene. The fact that I sit down to join them, even reluctantly, shows that I am beginning to notice and give some atten-tion to my inner child. The same 'mischievous child' reappeared in the following dream:

Church mischief

> I am lining up with other clergy outside a huge church to process in. It is for the funeral of an important person. I'm not quite sure who is taking the lead – we all seem to be involved. Then Katie, who is with us, misbehaves and runs off into the church ahead of us.

It is a very formal occasion, demanding the utmost decorum, and in rushes the impish child to disrupt the dignified proceedings. You can imagine the sense of dismay and embarrassment. Yet, even in the face of death, life cannot be restrained. It is the opposite of death. In both of these dreams, the mischievous child represents the anarchic, free spirit aspect of myself. I might try to control it but it is uncontrol-lable! She is the symbol of life that cannot be contained. Rather than trying to dampen it, I need to integrate it into my life. Perhaps the child needed to behave so outrageously in order to command my atten-tion! To become aware of our own inner child means we will be able to live life more naturally and spontaneously.[30]

Asper's research led her to conclude that the child in dreams is a symbol of life in general.[31] In cases where people are suffering from depression, the child symbol becomes connected with the denial of life. It is characteristic of the depressed to dream of dead children, who represent the cessation of everything living. The dead child in dreams is thus 'a symbol of life-denial, the negation of the will and the capa-city to live'.[32] Of course, as ever, it is important to know the life con-text of the individual. One grandmother had a frightening dream that her grandson was dead, but in that instance it was symbolic of the threat of her relationship with him being cut dead through the marital difficulties of the parents. For those who are suffering from severe depression, the life instinct becomes swallowed up in the death instinct. Hence, the dead child is a most powerful symbol of this. If and when there comes a point in which the depression draws towards an end, dreams of relating to a living child, especially one new-born, are common and are symbolic of a new beginning.[33]

The child motif can represent new beginnings arising from many different instances. One woman had this dream:

> I was walking on a path in the mountains, perhaps because I grew up near the mountains, and there were people walking . . . I was heading towards somewhere, not knowing where . . . there were two people in front of me. I didn't know who they were to start with but then I overtook them and saw these people were the parents of a friend of mine . . . I overtook them and found myself alone on this path. Then at some point ahead of me were my parents, my mum and my dad together. I went up to them; they turned around when I approached them and they were holding a little girl . . . and they passed her to me. Nothing was said.

She was very clear about what the dream might mean for her:

> There was a very positive feeling in the dream and a sense of purpose. The idea was that I was now taking care of this girl that they had been taking care of. There was a feeling of achieving something . . . a sense of closeness and harmony with them . . . The little girl could mean two things – it probably means myself as a child but not only in the past. It is that child which is in myself which is frightened, which is worried, which doesn't want to have lost the parents. My parents were in a way saying to me: now you can take care of her because you have grown beyond this stage of being frightened and worried. Alternatively it could be a child that I will have and my parents are saying that we have looked after you and now you have to look after a new life. The two are linked because before you can become a parent you must be a parent for yourself.

She interpreted the dream as a symbol of her independence now her parents were no longer there for her (deceased). The strong link with them had to be broken. She felt that she was now getting there and this is what her parents wanted for her. The dream is significant from the perspective of the grief process as it shows that she had come to terms with the death of her parents and was ready to move on in life. A couple of years later, she did in fact give birth to a daughter and has now ably taken on the role of the parent for herself.

A stage in life in which people often reassess their life goals is midlife. Jung conceptualized life as continually renewing itself[34] and this is manifest in our dreams. Asper writes, 'In this situation of new psychological orientation it is not uncommon for people – especially women – to dream about children.'[35] It is a time when responsibilities at home and work may be changing. People are both conscious of the approach of the end of life and desirous not to waste the time left. Midlife is a fitting time to discover some unrealized potential and try out something new. Dreams demand that we take ownership of the new life at hand.

> The dream child reveals to the dreamer . . . forgotten feelings of awakening that bring new zest . . . The dream child asks of us different attitudes. No doubt this involves an orientation towards the end of life; however, this orientation – and therein lies the contradiction – is at the same time new life.[36]

A woman at this stage in life had the following sequence of dreams, which she recalls in her own words.

Dream 1: Restored to life; Madonna and child; Drawing out the truth

> I am sitting at a table in a vast space with a very high roof – a barn or a church or cathedral. Around me is darkness except for a light shining on me and the table. I am drawing an image of the Madonna on paper, in pencil. Then I add the child, but where he comes from I'm not sure, a laughing, plump baby, cradled in her arms. As I finish drawing, the image starts to move and comes to life and is suffused by a golden glow. As I watch, the Madonna lifts the baby to her shoulder. He bounces up and down with delight and stretches his arms out to me. As the image fades, I feel astonished and joyful.

Dream 2: Lost; Angel deprivation

> I feel as if I am swimming and trying not to drown, but I'm really walking in thick fog, trying to find my destination – the right house or the right way. I hear a voice telling me not to be so impulsive; it tells me I am suffering from sleep deprivation, which I somehow know is really angel deprivation. Then I see the colour yellow or gold and know it means new beginnings.

Dream 3: The spiral; Vortex

I can see a spiral in front of me. It is still at first – then starts to move, changing into a whirlwind shape and back again to a spiral. I know this image is very important but I don't know why.

Dream 4: The fountain in the garden; Going with the flow

I can see a circular, classically designed fountain, standing in a large square basin in a garden at dusk – all around is very still. I can see and hear the sound of water falling into the basin.

The dreamer had experienced a fairly lengthy period of illness, which knocked her self-confidence. She also compared herself unfavourably in relation to others in her Roman Catholic church, who exhibited a pious lifestyle and appeared to be so much more 'holy' than she was herself. By contrast, she was much more down-to-earth, approachable, empathetic and discerning – qualities, it turned out, that were eminently suited to the ministry of spiritual direction, a course of training which she was just about to embark upon. Already an artist and a poet, she was a very creative person but was blighted by some self-doubt. The first dream came as an invitation to recognize her latent potential and exercise her new gift.

The child in the drawing comes to life, signifying her own new venture. But this is no ordinary inner child dream – it has a spiritual dimension. The setting appears to be a religious building, symbolizing the dreamer's spiritual Self. Darkness and light are in stark contrast and the dreamer is markedly in the 'light'. The child is the Christ child, offering divine blessing for her creativity. In contrast to the sobriety of her fellow church-goers, the child is happy and laughing. There is a sense of lightness and freedom. The child welcomes the dreamer with open arms and offers her the gift of joy. Asper says of the Divine Child,

> The Divine Child . . . is a psychic model that mediates to the individual the idea of the comprehensive and transpersonal character of the child principle. Such a principle cannot be fully integrated; it exceeds the human dimension. When it appears in dreams, it points to something new and gently balances out old and rigid modes of experience and well-worn thinking patterns.[37]

The subsequent dreams also have a spiritual quality to them and reinforce the theme of new beginnings. The second dream illustrates that finding the right path is not always straightforward. There are 'fogs' which blind and confuse along the way. For the dreamer, the fog symbolized emptiness. Through meditating upon the dream, she learnt that during such 'empty' times she needed to learn patience and accept the gift of stillness. In the third dream, the spiral is an archetypal form that is woven into the fabric of the universe, from the shape of galaxies to the DNA helix. It is associated with the cyclic patterns of growth and development of the psyche.[38] In a dialogue with the spiral, the dreamer learnt that the spiral was indeed a symbol of movement and change and moving on. It came for her to go deeper and to understand. It voices, 'If you can risk the spiral journey, I will always bring you back to the centre.' It offers the gifts of wisdom and discernment. In the final dream, the garden is reminiscent of the mythological Garden of Eden. Instead of a Tree of Life, there is a Fountain of Life. In the Christian tradition, water is a symbol not only of life but also of eternal life. The circular shape of the fountain reinforces this, as the circle is a symbol of eternity – life, which has no end. The fountain is 'the source of all life'. The dreamer is invited to 'flow with the fountain' and to 'water the garden'. Thus, the dreamer is called to participate in the task of bringing spiritual life and refreshment to others through her future ministry of spiritual direction.

Remembering that the Self contains the image of God, the Divine Child is the most outstanding form in which the Self appears in dreams because the child, being alive, challenges us and necessitates orientation towards the future. Careful attention is required, because unlike other symbols for the Self we do not know the exact content of the Divine Child. We need to remain open and respond with unconditional love to this symbolic child.[39] However, Asper cautions that the ideal qualities with which we endow the child, such as innocence, spontaneity and harmony, are those that belong to the Divine Child, from which we need to distinguish ourselves. The Divine Child can never be integrated; it can only be reflected in us, as we strive for those ideals.[40]

In the previous chapter, we learnt that death in dreams is associated with transformation and new beginnings. It is unsurprising, then, that the symbol of the child is also found in the realm of death. The appearance of the child motif in the dreams of those who are approaching death represents a new stage of change. It illustrates the age-old concept of death as new birth. The ancients used to bury their dead curled up in a foetal position, expressing the idea that 'human beings, born as children, in death return to the primordial ground of creation as children once again'.[41] In the Christian faith, death marks the passage from temporal, corporeal life to eternal life with Christ. The Anglican funeral service characteristically commences with the sentence from Scripture: 'I am the resurrection and the life . . . Those who believe in me, even though they die, will live, and everyone who lives and believes in me will never die' (John 11.25, 26).

Creative dreaming

All dreams are creative by virtue of their imaginative self-expression. However, there are some dreams that exhibit a real ingenuity as a source of artistic inspiration or in offering solutions to problems. The work of the Surrealists, in particular, is influenced by their dreams: for instance, Salvador Dali's famous painting of soft watches, *The Persistence of Memory*, stemmed from a dream about runny Camembert.[42] In the supposedly more rational side of life, many great scientific discoveries and inventions have resulted from dreams. The basis of Einstein's theory of relativity came from a dream that he had when he was a teenager. In the dream he was sledging with his friends at night. On one of the downward slides, he began to travel so fast that he realized he was approaching the speed of light. He looked up and saw the stars, which were being refracted into a spectrum of colours that he had never seen before, and he was filled with a sense of awe and numinosity. Einstein knew that somehow he was looking at the most important meaning in his life.[43] The invention of the sewing machine by Elias Howe is a novel example. After wrestling with the design for some considerable time, Howe had a terrifying dream in which he was being chased by cannibals. He was caught and put into a huge cauldron of boiling water. Every time he tried to pull himself out of the pot, the natives poked him back in again with their sharp spears. When Howe awoke from his 'nightmare', it suddenly dawned on him that the spears had holes in their pointed end! This was the brainwave he had been racking his brains for; the needle in the sewing machine needed to have the hole in the sharp end and not the blunt end as in conventional sewing. Interestingly, this dream also qualifies as a 'Shadow' dream. The creative solution to the technical problem is in the hands of the darkest, most frightening figures in the dream. This is a prime example of the positive value of 'nightmares'. We need the courage to face what scares us most in order to see the creative possibilities.[44]

Someone studying the subject of discernment, in the light of the Ignatian Spiritual Exercises, wrote:

> In my dreams I wrestled with understanding the subject of Discernment as a linear mathematical model that would encompass my feelings of frustration! Then I was confronted with the image of 'The Great Wave' and I instantly knew it was the answer to 'Discernment'! . . . Since then I have taken the image to reflection and prayer and allowed the image to speak to me of the still depth of God's love and peace in the noise of the surface turmoil.

Not only did the dream provide a creative 'solution' but it then fed the dreamer's own conscious creativity as she captured it in the following poem.

Night Wave

Hokusai's Great Wave unfolds,
its awesome power of
frustrated passion unleashed.

The flimsy plans of
my barques, buckle,
buffet and are breached.

Now Morning Star is hid.
Dawn holds the lightening sky,
where schemes lay storm-dashed.

Home calls me on,
yet its chilling snow and dangerous fire within,
alarms, perturbs, dismays.

Deep and deeper still.
A way is found
beneath the passion's foam.

No white froth here.
The rich thick water swirls
purple, violet, blood red.

Temple water of majestic weight.
Healing Oil, fractals of light,
I float on heaven's tide.

In His converging ways,
where safety had seemed unlikely,

> I dare to spiral deep
>> and
>>> sleep.

Clearly then, being open to our dreams can unleash our creative instincts. If you have exhausted all the conscious avenues for solving a problem, do not rule out finding an answer in your dreams. Creativity works best when vertical and lateral thinking are combined. First, the vertical conscious logical process absorbs all the data, and then the unconscious mind consolidates and incubates the information, working laterally to come up with a creative solution.[45] How incredible that we can have some of our most creative and productive thoughts when we are asleep! Note that such dreams are still symbolic and require thinking through, as any other dream. Various works have been produced on creativity, such as Gordon Lamont's book *The Creative Path* (see the Bibliography for details), in which he explores some ways of tapping into our own creativity, including dreams.

Prospective or pre-cognitive dreams?

> Dreams may sometimes announce certain situations long before they actually happen. This is not necessarily a miracle or a form of precognition. Many crises in our lives have a long unconscious history. We move toward them step by step, unaware of the dangers that are accumulating. But what we consciously fail to see is frequently perceived by our unconscious, which can pass the information on through dreams.[46]

A tiny percentage of dreams fail to conform to the standard rules of dream interpretation – that the dream is a symbolic portrait of the subjective world of the dreamer and does not correspond literally to external events. Certain dreams actually draw our attention to a possible future reality, and the significance of the dream may not become apparent until after the event. It is only in hindsight that such a dream can be verified in this futuristic light. It is rare for individuals to have such dreams, but when you add up all those who have had such seemingly predictive dreams, there is a sufficient number to merit some notice. What are we to make of this? How, indeed, is it possible? One view is to see the dream as *prospective*: that is, anticipatory of future events, as in the above quote by Jung. On this understanding, such dreams are not prophetic, they are 'merely an anticipatory combination of possibilities which may coincide with the actual behaviour of things'.[47] Alternatively, we could regard the dreams as *pre-cognitive*, in some way prophetic or telepathic. In fact, Jung's experience also led him to accept the influence of telepathy on certain dreams. Some people are more sensitive to it than others. However, he had no simple explanation for it and allowed for different possibilities.[48] Taylor looks to the concept of 'synchronicity' to describe events (and correspondingly in dreams) which, though seemingly random, are also symbolically resonant with other events in waking life. Such experiences are apparently inexplicable in causal terms.[49] As a result, Taylor has called into question the notion of the immutability of the flow of time from the past into the future and believes that '"synchronicity" is a consequence of the ultimate unity of all phenomena'.[50] Taylor also holds on to the likelihood of apparently pre-cognitive dreams also having personal symbolic value for the dreamer.[51]

There is much that we do not understand about the unconscious and the collective unconscious. I wish to remain open about the 'how' and focus on the 'why' of these forward-looking dreams. From what I can gather, prospective or pre-cognitive dreams have a purpose to either warn or encourage us. We should always handle such dreams critically, with caution. To date, I am aware of having one dream of this nature. It was meaningless to me at the time but jumped out at me a year later when I was skimming through my dream journal. It is recalled below:

> I am at a social function in a large living-room area with comfy armchairs. A woman comes in, whom I do not really notice or recognize at first. She has a scarf wrapped around her head. She comes up to me and says that I took her wedding a couple of weeks ago and makes a reference to one of her young children. The penny drops and I see the resemblance in her, although she does look rather altered. Then she begins to confide in me that the marriage has not been working. She is talking as though it is completely failed already after such a short space of time. She intimates that her husband is behaving differently. I want to draw her attention to all the years together before they married – it seemed to work then. I see the need to counsel her about it but then we are interrupted and one of us is whisked away.

This dream occurred the night before I officiated at a wedding. Upon waking, I was somewhat fazed by the dream. I recorded it but did no further work on it. It just made no sense. It did not seem to relate to my own life context. It was not as if my husband and I had

had a row recently. It never occurred to me that the dream might relate to the wedding I was due to take that day. The couple I was marrying had been rather over-anxious about the ceremony and particularly demanding of my time in the run-up to the wedding, but I had viewed that as pre-wedding nerves and had no concerns about the strength of their relationship. They had been together for several years and had already weathered some of life's trials together. They appeared to be very devoted to one another. However, my unconscious apparently thought otherwise! A year later, I got chatting to the groom's parents at a social function. Upon enquiring about the happy couple, I got a rather sheepish response. It transpired that the groom had left the marital home some months earlier. The marriage had failed. I had obviously picked up some disquiet about the relationship on an unconscious level. My conscious Self had dismissed it as a rather ridiculous dream that I had no time or inclination to work on there and then. Had I thought otherwise, there would have been little I could have done about it at that stage. Imagine the headlines: 'Priest refuses to marry couple because of troubling dream'. I don't think so!

My father had a more dramatic dream while on a family visit in America. He writes:

> I was in a London double-decker bus and we were travelling at far too high a speed and went into a tight right-hand bend. The bus went on to the two near-side wheels and the roof caught the top of a roadside bus shelter and demolished it! It went on to hit a barrier on the left side and then I woke up.

He described the dream to his sister at breakfast that morning, and then nothing more was thought of it. At noon the same day, he was being driven, with his sister, by his brother-in-law from Saratoga to New York down the Taconic Parkway. While travelling about 60 mph, his brother-in-law suddenly took a slip road to the right. It had a maximum speed of 25 mph and was a tight, 180 degree turn back on themselves. My father instinctively yelled at him to brake. They slid sideways, tipping on to two wheels, into the crash barrier and slid along it. The car was wrecked but they were unharmed apart from tattered nerves! However, had my father not reacted in time, they would have gone over the top of the barrier and met their fate in the wooded valley below. The dream served to sharpen my father's instincts and probably saved their lives.

In both of these dreams, the details do not precisely match the life situations they forewarn of, but the plot is essentially the same. In reality it was the groom's parents I encountered at the social function and the bride's distress was implicit through them. My sense of incredulity was the same, as was my internal dialogue about the significant number of years they had been together prior to marriage. In my father's dream, the scenario of a fast-travelling vehicle turning sharply around a very tight bend, turning on to two wheels and then hitting a crash barrier was identical. However, his unconscious had translated the incident to a familiar scene from his past. The fact it was a double-decker bus highlights the instability of the vehicle.

Another contact also shared two prospective, or pre-cognitive, dreams. One took place before the summer of 1992, before she met her husband. She was alone on a boat, leaving a harbour behind and going towards another place, she did not know where but she felt happy to go there. It was night and very dark, which resembled things being unclear, but she could see the lights of the land ahead. Upon waking she felt very positive. This feeling came back to her years later at the time of her wedding and she remembered the dream. (She travelled overseas to marry.) She linked the dream to that particular event. She thought it was difficult to say whether the dream was actually foretelling the future but it certainly seemed to refer to it. The other dream was less palatable. It occurred in 1996, before the death of her mother. It was a very disturbing dream about her mother being ill. Some months after, her mother was diagnosed as having cancer and the final stages of her illness corresponded exactly to the dream picture. The dream warned and prepared the dreamer for what was to come.

The ultimate goal – individuation

You will recall from Chapter 1 that *individuation* concerns the integration of the personality. It is 'a movement toward consciousness of the total inner Self', which entails bringing the inner dream personalities into a synthesis.[52] In concrete terms, this means fulfilling our own potential and becoming a person in our own right. This wholeness of our total being is expressed in the archetype of the Self and the Self is also the principle of integration.[53] Dreams connect the ego with the Self, both the centre and the totality of our personality. Our full potential is only truly realized when it is accompanied by the development of consciousness as a result.[54] Jung observed that successive dreams, over a long period of time, transpire to have a planned goal in mind, all forming part of the individuation process.[55] In addition to this underlying motive of all the 'little dreams', there are the 'big' dreams that give a snapshot summary of the individuation process. Some years ago, I had the following dream:

> I am standing beside an indoor swimming pool which conveys the sense of being outside as there is a mist rising off the water. I want to swim but am unprepared, without a swimming costume. I resolve to swim in the leggings and fleece top that I am wearing (over a 'crop top' style sports bra). I dive into the water. It is ice cold. I gasp for breath as I begin to swim with all my might. Although I am a strong swimmer, I quickly start to sink as my fleece absorbs the water. I panic as I slip beneath the surface. I look upwards and see the light reflecting on the surface of the water above me. I know that I will not ascend again until I remove the fleece top. I struggle in the water and manage to get rid of the top. I float up to the surface and proceed to lap up and down the pool, unhampered.

I have come to regard this as metaphor of my individuation. The dream occurred in a transitional phase of my life. From a Jungian perspective, I have descended into my own depths, water being 'a living symbol of the dark psyche', the unconscious.[56] Struggling in the water could indicate a fear of being engulfed by hidden unconscious forces and that my control over the unconscious needs to be relaxed gently. I should not be fighting against the unconscious but allowing myself to be submerged in it at a time and rate such that I can cope with what its depths disclose. The fleece represents the things, either material, relational or aspects of my personality, which need to be cast off in order for me to float again. The dream ends positively; I will emerge and swim again. Significantly, my rising to the surface of the water mirrors the Self, rising through the layers of consciousness during individuation.

The next dream was described by the dreamer as a 'master dream'. It is a key dream that has continued to unfold throughout her life and marks the beginning of the road that she is now on. She describes it as 'a whole story of transformation; it was a much deeper answer to my problem ... and my quest ... The dream was saying, "It's in you, all of this is in you." '

> I was in the car with my husband ... we pulled into this cement multi-storey car park ... really ugly and grey and bleak and dirty and black

and cold, just barren and just – ugh – horrible place. I needed to go to the loo . . . I get out and I'm kind of wandering and lost and I can't find the loo and this man who was an Indian . . . tall, elegant, exotic man just knew what I was looking for and just pointed . . . I follow his directions and I come into this hallway going down a slope and it's all mosaic-ed . . . all images of Victorian bathrooms . . . quite art nouveau and very attractive . . . but it wasn't a loo. Instead, there was a trap door and so I went into this trap door and immediately, instead of being in this awful car park, I'm in this huge mansion and I drop down and there was a real sense of quietness and awe. I was in this really enormous beautiful, rich, plush, ornate, fantastic mansion. I plonked into the dining room. The dining room was huge and had really thick blue carpet and I saw all the paintings on the wall and this huge, huge table with candelabra and silver and goblets and this beautiful furniture and a chandelier and candles burning and it was all set out for this huge banquet and it was utterly, utterly quiet. There was almost a sense of holiness . . . I had a sense of trespassing but at the same it was really nice to be there. I went into the next room . . . it was this huge square room . . . like a drawing room. It was all decorated in red and gold. The walls were red with lots of gilt frames. It was Louis XIV furniture. Against the back wall, sitting utterly quiet and still, was a whole orchestra, and they were sitting on red velvet upholstered chairs . . . Queen Anne chairs . . . and they were dressed in red and white and gold – Hungarian national costumes, which is interesting for me because I am half-Hungarian . . . they were just waiting, poised . . . and for some reason, I knew that the woman sitting . . . on the second to the end of the front row on the right . . . and she was about my age . . . I knew she was the leader . . . she had that kind of authority about her. I went up to her and I said (I was very apologetic), 'I'm lost, I'm so lost, I don't know what to do.' She doesn't address that at all but she stands up in a very business-like and brisk manner and starts to tell me about the orchestra and how the orchestra could play any kind of music in the entire world . . . this total variety, sometimes we would be Chinese, today we were Hungarian, other times we might be Arabic . . . she was very in charge and full of life, she was the opposite of me, she knew what she was doing and she had this total range of creativity . . . but she was just one of the group . . . Then she guided me . . . led me out . . . into the hallway, and the hallway had big, big wooden stairs and I knew the owners of the house were upstairs and I knew they were like an elderly royal couple. She took me to the hallway where there was a big carved wooden chest and it was alarmed . . . and inside this huge chest there was only one thing and it was a big key, a wooden carved key and . . . she gave it to me and she just motioned where to go and I left and I went outside the house and there I was back in the car park, with all the bare cement . . . I thought, I have no idea where I am . . . I'm totally disorientated . . . then . . . I could see our car and he was nudging his way through the traffic to find me and I knew he would find me and I felt very, very loved.

The dream occurred at a bleak time in the dreamer's life, indicated by the opening unattractive scene. To search for a toilet, in dreams, is characteristic of the need for self-expression, for either creative or cathartic reasons (symbolized by what comes out of us). As it transpired, the dreamer had an abundance of creative potential that was waiting to be released. The fact that she never found a toilet in the dream may indicate a conflict, at that point in time, between her need to express herself and the fear of doing so. However, what she did discover was astounding and set her on her path to self-fulfilment. Everything in the house is taken to be representative of the dreamer's soul, and the Indian, the dreamer's Animus, is right on cue to show the way. As explained in the last chapter, the Animus can play a very significant role in a woman's individuation process. In the dream, he points the way to the collective unconscious, and consequently to the development of her intellectual and spiritual side. The orchestra represents the collective unconscious and relates to the creativity in her Hungarian background. It was as though her own creativity was on hold and she needed to own that wealth of creativity; the banquet was waiting to happen. This included being open to the presence of God. The key related to her faith, reinforced by the sense of holiness in the hall. It was an honour to be given the key that she had not asked for. The challenge was to be unafraid, to be like the conductor woman. The dreamer had to own that richness: 'There was the sense that the woman who led the orchestra was me; she was the me that I was meant to be.' The dream is now a living reality accompanied by a sense of grace and richness from God. The dreamer concluded: 'I feel like an orchestra in my life.'

Conclusion

What an incredible journey dreams can take us on, from healing past pain and addressing personality issues to realizing the potential of the future. Sometimes the journey may be a slog, fraught with difficulties, and at other times we may be flying over the mountain tops. However, all dreams orientate us in the direction of personal progress even if it may feel as though we are taking a detour at the time. We can learn so much about ourselves. A commitment to dreamwork also means a commitment to personal growth, entailing personality change and development.[57] This means establishing a strong ego–Self relationship in the personality. The Self cannot fulfil its function of integrating the personality without the help of the ego, because the ego is what makes us conscious of reality. As such, the ego has to relate to the inner and the outer world.[58] Through dreams, we can become not only unconsciously but also consciously aware of our situation in order to make determined choices for the better.

In an article for the *Church Times*[59] about facing our inner contradictions and psychological defences, Simon Parke concluded the following, a fitting end to this chapter:

> My psyche is a battlefield after the war. There is scarred ground, the lingering smell of gunpowder, but a certain amount of peace there. Some figures lie dead, others wounded and groaning. Some stagger dazed and alone, while others gather around small fires for company and hot coffee. There are no enemies now. The shrill commands of confident leaders echo no more across my valley, and proud songs of battle are put away for good. Instead, I look to the horizon, possessing nothing but my wounds – and feeling strangely well.

6

Dreamwork

So difficult is it to understand a dream that for a long time I have made it a rule, when someone tells me a dream and asks for my opinion, to say first of all to myself: 'I have no idea what this dream means.' After that I can begin to examine the dream.[1]

No sixth sense is needed to understand dreams.[2]

There are a variety of approaches to working with dreams, some more involved than others. Jung had no fixed method of dream interpretation; he believed that it should be the result of mutual reflection and agreement by the dreamer and the analyst. In fact, it is impossible to work out the meaning of a dream without the collaboration of the dreamer except in very special circumstances.[3] Russ Parker, for one, is rather dismissive of working with dream symbolism and prefers to major upon the feeling content of the dream, using feelings as the 'drawbridge' between the dream and corresponding events in daily life.[4] While I agree that dream feelings are very significant, it strikes me as a little over-simplistic to rely upon feelings to yield the full meaning of the dream. We are not always aware of how we felt. I have a friend who has vivid dreams but who swears she rarely feels anything in them. There are no shortcuts in working with dreams if we are to arrive at a valid interpretation. Sometimes it requires some hard graft. The beauty of dreams is that any layperson can work with them, but it does help to know some tools of the trade. At first the dream may appear baffling, even to the likes of Carl Jung. However, in time, with a suitable approach, the meaning of the dream will become apparent – usually! Patience is a virtue in the field of dreamwork.

Most people do not have the luxury of working on their dreams with a therapist, but even if you do it is most beneficial to have done some work of your own on the dream first. I will therefore outline a basic method for working alone with dreams that can also be adapted to working with another person. It is a Jungian-based approach, with some embellishments. I will then offer some additional techniques and look at the dynamic of working with others on their dreams. Jung stressed that, until we learn otherwise, we have to treat dreams analytically.[5] However, it does not follow that dreamwork is straightforwardly a matter of analysing data in an objective way, nor is it a linear process. Kathrin Asper writes:

> A specific attitude is necessary to understand dreams. I would describe it in the following way: it circles rather than going in a straight line, waits rather than heading directly toward a goal; it consists more in *being* with the dream than in *having* the content of the dream; it accompanies the contents of a dream.[6]

Dreamwork, done well, is time consuming. If you tend to remember a lot of dreams it would be unrealistic to expect to do in-depth work on them all, unless you have all the time in the world at your leisure! The best compromise is to single out the seemingly most important dreams and give those quality time and attention. These are the dreams that leave more of a lasting impression on us, those containing images that stand out and that leave us feeling anxious upon waking. They may also be recurrent dreams, or it may be that the issues presented are also there in the other dreams. Usually, we have more significant dreams preceding or during special occasions and transitional points in our lives, such as starting a new job, getting married, during illness, starting therapy, going on retreat and even at major religious festivals. It is still worthwhile writing down all the dreams that you recall, irrespective of whether you have the opportunity to work on them or not, as this will give you a sense of your overall dreaming patterns. If you do record all your dreams, this does at least give you the option of coming back to any one of them in the future when you have the time and can see their significance in relation to other dreams. Until a dream message has been recognized and resolved, we will continue to have dreams about it. This means that it is not the end of the world if you miss some dreams, as you will continue to be bothered by the dream theme until you give it the attention it demands!

Preparation

Many people complain of not being able to remember their dreams in the first instance. So, before we dive into the dreamwork itself, there are a few preliminaries which will help with dream recall.

- Have a right intention. Before you even go to sleep, determine to remember a dream. You may even see fit to pray that you will remember one. I like this rather cute prayer:

> Dear God
> We give you thanks for the darkness of the night
> where lies the world of dreams.
> Guide us closer to our dreams so that we may be nourished by
> them.
> Give us good dreams and memory of them
> so that we may carry their poetry and mystery into our daily
> lives.
> Grant us deep and restful sleep that we may wake refreshed
> with strength enough to renew a world grown tired.
> We give thanks for the inspiration of stars,
> the dignity of the moon and the lullabies of crickets and frogs.
> Let us restore the night and reclaim it as a sanctuary of peace,
> where silence shall be music to our hearts
> and darkness shall throw light upon our souls.
> Good night. Sweet dreams. Amen.[7]

- Upon waking, lie still for a few moments concentrating on the dream impression, to allow the mood and details of the scene to come into clearer focus. (You may have to turn off your early morning news bulletin if it distracts!)
- Keep a dream journal by the bed. (Or at least a notepad to make rough notes that you can write up in your journal or file later.)
- Have a bedside lamp, or at least a torch if a lamp is not an option (for instance, when staying away from home or if a lamp would disturb someone else).
- If you still fail to bring any dreams to awareness when you awake, then a more anti-social approach may be required in the interests of progress. Set your alarm clock an hour before you usually wake up, at the time you will be having more extended phases of REM sleep. You should be stirred into consciousness in the middle of a dream. The dream will be interrupted but at least, after a few attempts at this, it should establish a pattern of bringing dreams into consciousness. Then, hopefully, you can return to normal times of waking, with greater dream awareness. Warning: this is not advisable if you share your bed with anyone, unless they are a particularly heavy sleeper, if you cherish the relationship!

Recording the dream

- Write the dream down immediately in the present tense, in as much detail as possible, without censoring or editing. The use of the present tense maintains the dream's immediacy and relevancy. The past tense distances the dream and serves to create a barrier between the waking mind and the dream experience.[8]

- Date the dream and leave sufficient space to work on it before the next entry.

- You may find it quicker and easier to tape record yourself recalling the dream first; a Dictaphone is useful for this. If you do so, still write it up in your journal later.

- If you *really* do not have time to write it up before getting out of bed, in the event that it will not go down well with the boss as an excuse for missing the train, then make a note of the date and one or two prompt words to help you record it at the earliest opportunity (on the train?!).

- Include the emotional tone of the dream: list all the feelings experienced in the dream and the emotional effect upon you on waking. Awareness of the mood of the dream will be advantageous when it comes to locating the dream in your own life situation.

- Make a note of your own life context. Are you at home or staying away somewhere? What has been going on for you in the previous days? Any significant events?

- Comment: note down any immediate thoughts or reactions. This could help when you come back to it if you are not doing the dreamwork there and then. If you do nothing further with it, you will have at least acknowledged the dream.

- Very occasionally, I find that a dream image surfaces during the day that I had not been aware of upon waking. It may occur when I am in the shower or even much later on in the day at a moment when my thoughts are free-floating. Watch out for this.

- While we might be eager for epic dream narratives, it is important not to dismiss dream fragments. Jeremy Taylor observes, "²am fragments, more often than not, reveal themselves to be ʳ condensed and "edited" versions of the night's dreaming."[9] ¹ only to remember fragments of dreams when our waking more frenetic.

The dreamwork itself

There are various steps to be taken before that 'eureka' moment of interpretation can be arrived at or even considered! A basic, thorough-going, seven-step approach is outlined below.

Step 1: 'Stilling' down

It helps to take a few moments to separate from daily life and quieten down so that we may be fully open and receptive to the source of the dream. Allocate yourself an uninterruptible amount of time that you know you can spend on working on the dream. Try to find a place in the house, or wherever you are, where you know you will be free from distractions. There are various centring techniques to still the mind and make us more present to the moment. These include breathing techniques and reciting mantras.[10] How about combining the two and saying to yourself 'Be' as you breathe in and 'still' as you breathe out? This can become a prayer in itself. It is taken from Psalm 46.10, 'Be still, and know that I am God.'

When you are ready, you might like to make a prayer of self-offering, such as the following adaptation of George Appleton's prayer by Jim Cotter.

> Give me a candle of the Spirit, O God, as I go down into the deeps of my being. Show me the hidden things, the creatures of my dreams, the storehouse of forgotten memories and hurts. Take me down to the spring of my life, and tell me my nature and my name. Give me free-dom to grow, so that I may become that self, the seed of which you planted in me at my making. Out of the deeps I cry to you, O God.[11]

Step 2: Identify the main theme and give the dream a title

Read through your initial dream account and add any further details that come to you. Sometimes we think of additional things in going over the dream again. As you regard the dream in its entirety, allow the main theme to emerge. There may be a secondary theme as well. Then you will be able to think of a title which captures the essence of the dream. Giving the dream a title assists with the overall cate-gorization of your dreams and easy reference. Your dream journal becomes 'like a photo album of inner psychic space'.[12] It also helps to get a sense of the dream as a whole. Once you have completed your dreamwork, you may choose to change the title!

Step 3: Amplification

For Jung the starting point for working on a dream is 'amplification': 'that is to enter into the atmosphere of the dream, to establish its mood as well as the detail of its images and symbols, in such a way as to *amplify the experience of the dream itself*'.[13] Amplification focuses on the dream symbols themselves and their inherent qualities. It is an objective, logical, left-brain activity that takes place in rational consciousness.[14] To carry out the process of amplification, first identify all the figures and objects in the dream, including places. Write them down, leaving space after each for the dreamwork. Taking each symbol in turn, ask: 'What are the particular characteristics and functions of this symbol?' i.e. 'What is it? What is its purpose?' Use a dictionary if necessary. Then ask yourself: 'What is the particular expression of this in the dream?' After listing all your thoughts, distinguish what would be *for you* the essential characteristic or function of the symbol at this particular time.

It may well be that some symbols have archetypal significance, with a universal meaning, but they will also hold a personal significance for you. Once you have recognized that a figure is an archetype, you need to go to the relevant source to see what it tells you about the archetype. J. E. Cirlot, *A Dictionary of Symbols* and C. G. Jung, *The Archetypes and the Collective Unconscious*, are helpful starting places (see the Bibliography for details). Subsequently, it may be beneficial to investigate the symbol further in its own mythical and/or religious context. For instance, for a character from Greek mythology, it would help to refer to a book on Greek myths. *Archetypal amplification*, then, is a process of gathering information about archetypes in dreams from sources such as myths, fairy tales and comparative religion.[15]

> Archetypal amplification begins with recognizing that an archetypal presence has entered into one's dream. The dream that contains an archetype often has a mythical quality. Instead of scenes that seem like the everyday world, the dream takes you to a place that feels ancient, from another time, or like a fairy tale. You find yourself in a legendary place like Baghdad in the time of genies, magic carpets, and magicians. Another sign is that things are bigger than life or smaller than life.[16]

Step 4: Making associations

While symbol amplification strives to be objective, symbol association is very much subjective. It helps to make conscious our own personal colouring of the dream symbols.[17] This stage needs to be quite painstaking. Looking at the first image, ask yourself: 'What are my associations with this symbol?' In other words: 'What things or expressions spring to mind in connection with it? What does it represent to me or remind me of? How does it make me feel?' List as many associations as you can until you are exhausted of ideas. The unconscious contains within itself the personal associations for all the symbols generated, therefore the symbolic language of dreams can be de-coded. This process is called *direct association* (to be distinguished from Freudian 'free-association' in which the mind drifts and the person says whatever comes into their head). Direct association is focused upon the symbol itself – keep coming directly back to the symbol each time. You might find it helpful to present your thoughts in a 'spider diagram', with the image central and all your associations radiating out of it.

Take each symbol in turn and repeat the same procedure until you have worked on all of the material. This might strike you as being a rather laborious process, but once you get the feel of it you will be surprised and energized by what comes up. Write down all your associations and do not censor them, even the ones that may seem too obvious, ridiculous or embarrassing. It is crucial that, as the dreamer, you record your own personal associations of the image. If you rush for a dictionary on symbols before you have done your own work you will never uncover the individual meaning that the dream has specifically for you. If there are any archetypal symbols, carry out the same process as with personal associations. Write down the associations that come to you from mythical sources and see which make sense. It is important to make a personal connection to the archetype; it is present in you, acting through you.[18]

Now you have done all the groundwork, you can choose the relevant association(s) for each image. This requires a more intuitive approach, dubbed by Jung the 'it clicks' method.[19] Simply go through each cluster of associations and, in the light of all the other symbols and associations, see which one seems to fit the big picture of the dream. There should be one association for each image that evokes something deep within you – it just feels right. Johnson says,

> One way to find the essence of a dream symbol is to go where the energy is – go to the association that brings up a surge of energy. Every symbol is calculated to rouse us, to wake us up. It is organically tied to energy systems deep in the substrata of the unconscious.[20]

Nevertheless, there may be times when it does not seem so obvious. If this is the case, do not force it but move on to the next symbol or even come back to the dream at another time. Occasionally, months have passed before I have fully figured out a dream that I have been working on! Leave it to incubate a while, but do not forget the dream altogether.

Step 5: Making connections

Once we have highlighted all our key associations, the next step is to discover what each represents in our inner lives. Taking each image in turn, ask: 'What aspect of me is this? When or where have I seen it recently?' Write down the connections made, giving specific examples from your life that correspond to the events in the dream.[21] On rare occasions (as we have seen in the instance of my dream about the failed marriage) a dream may relate to an external situation. However, as 99.9 per cent of the time dreams relate to our own lives – our inner dynamics – it is best to proceed initially on that assumption. It will eventually become clear if that is not the case. Even when we dream about those closest to us, frequently the dream figures will characterize that aspect of ourselves. Johnson writes,

> Every dream is a portrait of the dreamer. You may think of your dream as a mirror that reflects your inner character – the aspects of your personality of which you are not fully aware ... every trait portrayed in our dreams has to exist in us, somewhere, regardless of whether we are aware of it or admit it.[22]

Johnson also advises that a good way to connect to these inner parts of yourself is to regard each dream figure as an actual autonomous person living inside you. Then the question becomes: 'Where have I seen this person at work in my life lately? What part of me is it that feels, thinks and behaves like that?'[23] For example, if the dream person is in conflict, then try to identify the part of your personality that is in conflict or, if she or he is seeking relationship in the dream, look for that aspect of yourself. You may discern that she or he is a manifestation of one of the basic personality structures that make up the psyche, such as the Shadow or the Anima or Animus. The next task is to discover where the dream person is active in your life by writing a description of the person's main characteristics and what she or he means to you. Then look for the part of your personality that matches. It is best to get acquainted with dream personalities as individuals in their own right before sticking a universal label on them such as 'Anima' or 'Great Mother', if appropriate.[24] Even when working with archetypes, we need to establish how they relate to our own lives in the present. We have to ask: 'What does this archetype have to do with me individually?'[25]

Dreams disclose the unconscious beliefs and attitudes that motivate us and, subsequently, the unconscious patterns of behaviour generated by our inner attitudes. For each dream figure, it is pertinent to ask: 'What set of beliefs is this character functioning from? Do I hold the same opinions without realizing it?'[26] Dreams enable us to make a conscious choice, to accept or reject the attitudes in the dream or to make an intelligent synthesis,[27] which is the goal of individuation. As far as the unconscious attitude seems exaggerated, it will be compensating for the equally off-balance position of the ego in the opposite direction. Jung states, 'I make it a heuristic rule, in interpreting a dream, to ask myself: What conscious attitude does it compensate? By so doing, I relate the dream as closely as possible to the conscious situation.'[28] The final resolution should be somewhere between the unconscious and conscious positions.

It is paramount that you keep coming back to your own life situation and exploring how the dream relates to it. In Jungian therapy, it is customary to approach a dream in three stages: The **Personal Context** seeks to contextualize the dream in the life of the dreamer, to understand its personal significance. Second, the **Cultural Context** shows how the dream relates to the social surroundings and the time in which it was dreamt. Third, the **Archetypal Context** sets the dream in the historical context of human life as a whole. In practice it is seldom possible to keep these stages separate because they interact.[29] Ordinarily, the dream will correspond to recent events, but it is also possible for dreams to draw attention to unresolved issues in our personal and collective history. Often there is a stimulus in the present that resonates with the past (often painful) occurrence.

This stage of the dreamwork will be thoroughly complete only when we have carried out the process of making connections for all the animate and inanimate objects in the dream. Furthermore, do not overlook the feelings conveyed in the dream. Go back to your initial list compiled in the preliminary work and consider: 'When have I felt like that recently?' Feelings can be a powerful tool for connecting the dream to the life context that the dream alludes to. Then we can collate all the information and reach the stage we have all been waiting for . . .

Step 6: Interpretation

Now we come to the message of the dream. Finally you can consider the question: 'What is the meaning of the dream for my life?' Initially, spend a little time just 'being' with the insights of the previous stages as a whole. The interpretation should flow naturally out of the previous steps. The associations and connections begin to weave together and a sense of the dream's overall meaning emerges. Next, write down a coherent summary statement in response to the question: 'What is the central, most important message of this dream?' This statement may require a bit of rough drafting until it feels right. Keep working on it until it makes sense and fits into the overall pattern of the dream.[30]

> An adequate dream interpretation should sum up the meaning of your dream in a nutshell. It should also provide a specific application of the dream's message to your personal life, to what you are doing, to how you are going to live.[31]

The criterion for a true interpretation is having that inner recognition. In the event that you arrive at more than one seemingly correct interpretation for the dream, you need to decide which is the one that really 'clicks'. As before, look for the one with energy. Go with the interpretation that arouses energy and strong feelings in you and offers insights and liberates you from behaviour patterns you have been stuck in.[32] Johnson outlines four principles for validating interpretations:[33]

1 Choose an interpretation that shows you something you didn't know (or is repeating a message that do you already know but have failed to put into practice).
2 Avoid the interpretation that inflates your ego or is self-congratulatory.
3 Avoid interpretations that shift responsibility away from yourself.
4 Learn to live with dreams over time – fit them into the long-term flow of your life.

The fourth instance above relates more to those 'big' dreams that give 'a panoramic view of your inner development over a long period of time'.[34] The full meaning of such dreams becomes clearer over time. We have to patiently co-exist with these dreams, returning to them regularly until we see how the events of our lives fit the dream. To add a final waiver, without wishing to confuse or decry the importance of discovering the 'true' meaning for a dream, it is worth recognizing that dreams may be interpreted on different levels. Thanks to the multivalent nature of dream symbols, dreams can have more than one meaning. It is important not to be closed to the possibility of multiple meanings, but usually there is one that has the most pressing significance. The above guidelines would still apply in validating any secondary interpretations. Now the process is complete . . . almost . . .

Step 7: Do something in honour of the dream

This is the step that is likely to get overlooked. If our dreams are to make a genuine difference to our lives, it is important that we act upon our dreams concretely, that we engage our bodily Selves in giving heed to the lesson learnt rather than just acknowledging it at the cerebral level. Making a physical response enables the insights gained to become ingrained into our conscious lives and to become a living reality. The dream message is also grasped at a deeper level. Ask yourself: 'What am I going to do about this dream?' Your response could be a *practical* action: for instance, cutting down your workload and giving more time to relationships; or it could be a *symbolic* act, creating a ritual that powerfully reinforces the meaning of the dream.[35] Ritual forms a relationship between the conscious and unconscious minds; it takes the wisdom of the unconscious and imprints it upon the conscious mind.[36] To view ritual from a psychological standpoint, it could be described as 'symbolic behaviour, consciously performed'.[37]

The ritual does not have to be anything elaborate; often, the most effective rituals are small. It needs to be manageable. 'The ritual is a physical representation of the inner attitude change that the dream called for . . . The best rituals are physical, solitary, and silent: These are the ones that register most deeply with the unconscious.'[38] Ritual forms a significant part of religious ceremony and worship. It has been a natural part of human cultural and religious life since the most ancient of times. The Eucharist, for example, is a powerful symbol of Christian doctrine and unity. Through it we embody belief. Sadly, Western secular society has lost sight of the value of ritual as a necessary part of human existence. It has also been downplayed in Evangelical Christianity. We need to rediscover the importance and power of ritual in daily life. There is a growing hunger for ritual in worship, in evidence in new forms of worship springing up towards the end of the twentieth century, such as the 'Alternative Worship' movement, which rediscovered the riches of Catholic liturgical tradition and combined them with new contemporary forms of expression. The result is a creative postmodern eclectic mix with a real sense of reverence.[39]

We need to make rituals in order to get in touch with dream energy and divine energy within us all. Ritual is also one of the most appropriate channels to respond with a sense of awe and gratitude.[40] We should give thanks for dreams and not take them for granted. Always try to come up with a fitting response to your dream, even if you have to think about it for a few days. Some action, however simple, is always better than doing nothing.

Having a long-term view

Ultimately, dreams are part of the mystery of ourselves. Do not get over-concerned to pin down an interpretation that seems elusive. Let the meaning bubble up over time. In the long run, patterns will start to emerge; you will begin to pick out recurrent dream motifs and themes and these will point to the most important issues for you. This is where keeping a dream journal is imperative. Furthermore, your journal becomes a written record of your physical, mental, emotional and spiritual life story. Keep it safe and private! Always leave at least one blank page after every dream recorded in your journal. If you are not able to work on the dream then, you may well want to come back to it at some point in the future and it will be frustrating if there is no space for your dreamwork alongside the dream! Personally, I find it helpful to use Post-It colour index tabs to categorize my dreams under the major recurrent themes that run through my dreams – food, travel and baggage, water, fire, war and conflict, inner child, to name a few. These significant themes can be listed at the back of the journal with a colour-coded key for finding them. I can then pick one particular theme at a time and revisit all the dreams with that main theme. I find that some have been worked on fully, some half-worked and others abandoned completely, where I did not have the time or inclination to work on them. Often, in the light of the other similar dreams, it is then easier to look again at the unresolved dreams. As the big picture starts to become clearer, even the 'finished' dreams can end up with an altered or enhanced meaning.

It is really helpful to take stock every so often, for instance at the start of a new year or while on retreat, to carry out a 'dream life review'. Reflect upon the development and meaning of your major themes and issues, perhaps asking yourself: 'What has been most life-giving for me? What have I learnt about myself? Have I responded appropriately? Where have I been drawn to or away from God?' Summarize the most important insights and changes that have taken place in you. This then becomes a point from which to move forward with greater clarity.

Worked dream example

The following is an example of the seven-step approach at work on a dream that I had six months into my curacy in a fairly traditional liberal catholic–central Anglican benefice. The dream will be worked through from the perspective of that point in time.

> I am inside an old (medieval?) rural church building, which is a round shape. It is simply an inspection visit with a view to redecoration. The walls are deep red but mottled all over with thick black mould. I intend to paint over them with bright yellow paint. I groan inwardly at the immensity of the task as the walls will take a lot of scrubbing down and cleaning up before the new paint can be applied.
>
> There is another person with me (male?) but I don't know who it is. I am informed that the church is haunted. As I head towards the door to leave I am affronted by a somewhat cartoon-like ghost, resembling a long-handled string mop. It is darting about the place and laughing cheerfully. I am not really afraid but rather taken aback.

You may recall from Chapter 2 that dreams tend to have a fourfold narrative form, identified by Jung as: the statement of place; the development of the plot; the culmination; and the solution. In my dream, the first three parts are there but the fourth is missing. The scene is set with myself and a companion in the church; the plot develops as I notice the state of the place and plan to scrub the walls and repaint; then the culmination as the mop-ghost appears and startles me. The final result will need to be achieved through the dreamwork itself. Feelings entailed initial curiosity, a sense of reluctance at a tedious task ahead, then surprise at what happened next. Let us assume that we have done the first step of stilling down and move on to . . .

Step 2: Identify the main theme and give the dream a title

Redecoration appears to be a major theme in this dream. (Interestingly, I had a further dream a week later, also on the theme of redecoration, so this was a recurrent theme around that time.) Perhaps, though, the theme of transformation captures the sense of the whole dream. I have given the dream the title 'True Colours'.

Step 3: Amplification

THE OLD CHURCH – place of worship, building visited by tourists, pilgrims and ramblers, place of refuge and shelter, in this case it seems to have fallen into disuse and neglect = *place of worship in state of neglect.*

RURAL LOCATION – in the countryside, *off the beaten track.*

ROUND SHAPE – *spherical*, circular, *Eastern Orthodox* churches tend to be round (in contrast to the more masculine or phallic architecture of Western churches).

RED walls – *a bold bright colour.*

THICK BLACK MOULD – *fungal growth*, spreads and leads to decay if not treated, sign of neglect.

YELLOW paint – *bright sunny colour.*

MY (MALE?) COMPANION – *masculine figure who comes alongside = Animus?*

THE STRING MOP COMIC GHOST – a *cleaning tool* that could be used to clean up the walls. A mop is an inanimate object but this one is animate and full of life = *the Trickster archetype in one of its many guises?*

Step 4: Making associations

THE OLD CHURCH – religious building, work place, holy place, sacred space, *spiritual*, historic, ancient, communion of saints, *tradition.*

RURAL LOCATION – scenic, agricultural, backwater, *isolated*, forgotten about.

ROUND SHAPE – *feminine*, womb-like, containing.

RED walls – anger, *passion*, womb-like, *life-blood*, 'though your sins are like scarlet', danger, English rose.

THICK BLACK MOULD – left neglected, poor state of care, unattractive, needs a good scrubbing up, *conceals what lies beneath*, stale, musty, *'fit the mould'.*

YELLOW paint – 'bright sunny yellow', popular colour for painting
kitchens, daffodils, buttercups, *I dislike yellow as it is the colour I
see if I become dizzy and likely to faint.*

MY (MALE?) COMPANION – stranger, *reassuring and non-threatening
presence,* not alone, supportive, *there to advise?* I think the person
is *male.*

THE STRING MOP COMIC GHOST – cartoon-like, *mocking, playful,*
lively, alarming, incongruous; *cleaning tool* that is not abrasive like
a scouring pad or scrubbing brush.

The key amplifications and associations above have been italicized.
We now hold objective and subjective reflections together and take
each symbol in turn.

Step 5: Making connections

THE OLD CHURCH – Buildings are a symbol of the Self. The church
represents my spiritual Self – my public role in leading worship
and my inner spiritual state. It is a part of myself with a long history and sense of continuity with others through the ages. It also
has to do with my upholding tradition in worship, either in terms
of the style of worship and/or the conventions of the individual
churches where I take services.

RURAL LOCATION – I am feeling a bit isolated in my spiritual Self. I
am still mourning the loss of the theological college community
that was a source of spiritual sustenance and vitality for me. I feel
a bit like a coal flung out of the fire to go cold on my own.

ROUND SHAPE – This is my feminine Self, my source of creativity,
nurture and wisdom. I inhabit a professional world that is still
predominately male in structure and outlook. Although the church
feels like an English country church, the Eastern shape serves to
balance and challenge the more traditionally paternalistic, rationalistic values of the Anglican Church.

RED walls – This is the passionate part of me that makes me thrive.
It is to do with what gives me life.

THICK BLACK MOULD – The passionate part of me has become stale.
In my new parish context, I have allowed my essential spiritual Self
to become hidden behind a mask of conformity – I have felt obliged
to 'fit the mould'.

YELLOW paint – I see yellow, literally, 'when I am not feeling myself'.
This is the colour that I know everyone else likes and so I plan to

become that colour in order to please others. I am trying, through my public Persona, to become something that I am not, and this conceals what lies underneath. Worse still, the colour yellow is something that I find off-putting.

MY (MALE?) COMPANION – If, as I sense, the companion is male, he is likely to be my Animus. He acts as my soul guide to the areas of my unacknowledged inner potential.

THE STRING MOP COMIC GHOST – The Trickster archetype in mop-like guise. He mocks my pretensions to redecorate in a colour that I personally dislike. In other words, he comes to warn me of the folly of my actions in trying to become what I am not comfortable with being. At the same time he appears in the form of the equipment I need to be cleaned up and let my true Self be revealed. It is not to be done harshly, though. He is a symbol of transformation to restore me to life.

Step 6: Interpretation

The ancient feel to the location and the appearance of an inanimate object come to life gives the dream an archetypal quality, which makes it feel quite significant. The dream shows that, in the context of worship, I was losing my vitality. I was aiming to conform to expectations that were not life-giving for me. To fail to be true to my authentic Self spells danger. The dream comes as a warning that I need to let myself be seen in my true colours. It reminds me of the sound advice that I was given at my ordination: 'Be yourself.' The task ahead feels a little daunting; it could take a long time for my true Self to feel at ease emerging, but the tools are at hand. Rowan Williams' sermon at his enthronement as Archbishop of Canterbury gave me a jolt – it was like a confirmation of my dream! He said:

> God sees us in our true colours . . . We can only become completely human when we allow God to remake us. Like the conservationist in the art gallery, God works patiently to remove the dust and grime of ages and to let us appear in our true colours . . . it means also that God will lay bare all the ways that we hide from him and each other.

Step 7: Do something in honour of the dream

Despite the formal and traditional nature of the main parish, I am permitted a lot of freedom. The incumbent is supportive of my new ideas and initiatives (within reason!). Therefore, I should not regard myself as totally constrained by the set-up. I resolve:

- to retain something of myself in formal
  through the type of welcome I give and m'
  the service;
- to seek opportunities to lead more exper'
  ship, e.g. introduction of bi-monthly Alteⅰₙ.
  of Evensong.

With practice, the above process does speed up a little, as you beₐ.
to get more of a feel for working with symbols. So long as you complete all the stages it does not need to be set out in this way. I write
my amplifications, associations and connections alongside each
other for each symbol.

Other dream techniques

Dialogue with a dream figure or object

> Dialoguing with dream figures puts us in touch with both the invita-
> tion and the energy to change and grow.[41]

Frederick (Fritz) Perls gave greater freedom to working with symbols
by using the Gestalt method. This gives symbols a voice. The question is, if each symbol could speak, what would it say? Perls saw dreams
as an existential message, telling us where we are in relation to ourselves and the world around us. He sought to uncover the various
messages in the dream and bring them together to form a whole picture of the person.[42] It would be fruitful, if we had all the hours in
the day, to dialogue with all the symbols in a dream. Such work would
provide a very comprehensive picture of the dream and the dreamer's psychology. However, in practice, simply to pick a dominant symbol and concentrate on that will still yield good insights on the journey
towards wholeness.

The dream dialogue technique helps us to establish a relationship
with the energies in a dream. It combines both sides of the brain's
functioning – the logical and linear functions and the affective and
creative side. Since it is carried out meditatively, it is also particularly
powerful in releasing spiritual energy and wisdom.[43] We can dialogue
with anything in a dream. It may come more naturally to dialogue
with people but it is also valuable to dialogue with the other creatures and even inanimate objects. Objects in our dreams represent
energies in symbolic form, and so it is possible to personify these

.s. Newcomers to this technique sometimes fear that nothing will
_pen. Try to persevere and trust the process. Another concern
that what is said is only the dreamer's conscious or 'made up'
response; however, after a few exchanges between you and the dream
figure, you should begin to sense the difference between what is
coming from your conscious ego and what is coming from your
unconscious in the form of the dream figure.

Try the method outlined below:[44]

- Choose a dream symbol, either a figure, an object or an image that
  strikes you as important. It may attract or repel you.
- Set aside some time and go to a place where you will not be interrupted. Have a pen and paper to hand. Have a few initial questions ready, e.g. 'Why did you appear in my dream? What do you
  have to teach me? Why did you act that way in my dream? What
  gifts do you have for me? Please tell me why I am feeling x, y or z
  towards you.'[45]
- Allow yourself to relax and enter into a prayerful meditative state.
  Welcome God's presence and ask for guidance in the dream
  dialogue.
- In your imagination, recreate the dream scene and let the dream
  figure come alive again. If the dream symbol is an object, personify
  it, perhaps naming it, in a way that you can dialogue with it.
- Ask open questions. Picture yourself asking them to the dream symbol and let the dialogue flow. Write whatever response comes to
  you as the dream figure replies.
- Continue the dialogue, noting the questions and responses, until
  you feel there has been an insight or resolution or the dialogue
  comes to a natural end. It is worth asking one final question: 'Do
  you have anything else to tell me or give me?' in case anything has
  been left out.
- Thank the figure as you conclude the session.
- Afterwards, take a few minutes to reread the dialogue and reflect
  on what happened. Try to clarify the insights that have been communicated and what you will do with them.

In the previous chapter, in looking at the motif of the Divine Child,
we examined the dreams of a woman in midlife. The woman used
the dialoguing technique in her personal dreamwork. We will
now be privy to her dialogues with the key symbols. These help
to illustrate the method outlined above. Notice how she uses

personification to engage with the images in the last three dreams. The dreams are written again, with the dream dialogue for each below.

Dream 1: Restored to life; Madonna and child; Drawing out the truth

I am sitting at a table in a vast space with a very high roof – a barn or a church or cathedral. Around me is darkness except for a light shining on me and the table. I am drawing an image of the Madonna on paper, in pencil. Then I add the child but where he comes from I'm not sure, a laughing, plump baby, cradled in her arms. As I finish drawing, the image starts to move and comes to life and is suffused by a golden glow. As I watch, the Madonna lifts the baby to her shoulder. He bounces up and down with delight and stretches his arms out to me. As the image fades, I feel astonished and joyful.

Dialogue 1: Talking to the child

Why have you come?
To show you the way and teach you many things.
Who are you?
The light of the world.
What have I to learn from you?
Truth – and who you are.
Do you have a gift for me?
Joy.
I am astonished by you.
I **am** astonishing.
Is there anything else you wish to tell me?
Pray.

The dreamer thanks the Christ child and he hugs her.

Dream 2: Lost; Angel deprivation

I feel as if I am swimming and trying not to drown, but I'm really walking in thick fog, trying to find my destination – the right house or the right way. I hear a voice telling me not to be so impulsive; it tells me I am suffering from sleep deprivation, which I somehow know is really angel deprivation. Then I see the colour yellow or gold and know it means new beginnings.

Dialogue 2: Talking to the voice in the fog

Why have you come?
To teach you the way back.
Who are you?

Emptiness.
What have I to learn from you?
Patience.
Do you have a gift for me?
Stillness.
I feel a bit wary of you.
No need.
Is there anything else you wish to tell me?
Be still and know that I am God.

The dreamer thanks the dream and is told to go in peace.

Dream 3: The Spiral; Vortex

I can see a spiral in front of me. It is still at first – then starts to move, changing into a whirlwind shape and back again to a spiral. I know this image is very important but I don't know why.

Dialogue 3: Talking to the spiral

Why have you come?
I want you to go deeper and to understand.
Who are you?
I am the symbol of movement and change and moving on.
What have I to learn from you?
If you can risk the spiral journey, I will always bring you back to
   the centre.
Do you have a gift for me?
Wisdom and commitment.
I am intrigued by you.
I will show you a mystery.
Is there anything else you wish to tell me?
Dare – jump – risk!

The dreamer thanks the dream and is told 'the double helix is a spiral'.

Dream 4: The fountain in the garden; Going with the flow

I can see a circular, classically designed fountain, standing in a large square basin in a garden at dusk – all around is very still. I can see and hear the sound of water falling into the basin.

Dialogue 4: Talking to the fountain

Why have you come?
To bring you refreshment.

Who are you?
The source of all life.
What have I to learn from you?
Tranquillity and calm.
Do you have a gift for me?
Flow with me.
I feel soothed by you.
Then sleep now.
Is there anything else you wish to tell me?
Water the garden.
Do you mean Saint Teresa's garden of prayer or my garden?
Both.

The dreamer thanks the dream and she seems to hear the sound of water falling.

As you can see, the dreamer was open to hearing the dream message and able to surrender herself to the process to powerful effect. She still retained control of her conscious ego and had responsibility for making the process work but was able to give voice to the unconscious energies within herself. Such dialoguing is the beginning of transformation; it allows the energy released in the dream to be named, evaluated, integrated and brought into the choices and actions of everyday life.[46] I was amused by the instruction to water the garden in the last dream. Perhaps it shows that dreams are still grounded in reality!

Technically speaking, dialoguing with a dream image is a form of active imagination, a technique we will now examine more fully.

Active imagination

Active imagination is a special use of the power of the imagination that is not confined to dreamwork. In addition to working with dreams, Jung developed the use of active imagination with unconscious material as a path to the unconscious in itself. Imaginative contemplation of Scripture has long been established as a way of praying. Such prayer is not confined to the 'script' of the biblical text. The Spiritual Exercises of St Ignatius of Loyola, first published in 1548, have inspired many to actively engage in biblical scenes in their imagination as a present reality, to hear God's message to them today.

Within this context, we will look at active imagination specifically in relation to working with dreams but in a way that echoes that of imaginative contemplation of Scripture, inviting God into the process. This technique is of particular value for working on a dream for which there has been no resolution and the dreamer is 'left hanging'. It extends and moves the dream on. It is a valid approach as both the imagination and the dream come from the same source in the unconscious.[47] The essence of active imagination is conscious participation in the imaginative experience. It is active because the ego enters into the inner world and takes part in the drama in the individual's imagination (contrary to passive fantasy).[48] It requires a basic attitude of openness and a willingness to listen.

> Active imagination begins with the principle that you must respect the unconscious and realize that it has something valuable to contribute; therefore the dialogue must be one between two intelligent equals who respect each other.[49]

The approach:

- As above, find a place when and where you will not be disturbed.
- Pray for God's grace to be at work in the situation and welcome the Holy Spirit.
- Take some time to centre down. This is especially important for this type of dreamwork, so that you are properly disengaged from outside concerns and receptive to the dream. Relax. Slowly and deliberately let all tension, anxiety and frustration flow away. Let all thoughts and inner storms subside. Let your mind, heart, will and feelings become tranquil. Open yourself up to an awareness of God's presence.
- Recreate the dream in your imagination, in as much detail as possible. Find your own place in it.
- Allow the action in the dream to continue naturally and spontaneously where it left off. Interact with the dream symbols as you feel led. Say or do whatever comes into your mind that feels appropriate. If nothing seems to be happening to begin with, you could start by asking who a figure is and what she, he or it wants.
- Do not try to control or manipulate the events but go along with what happens. There is no pre-prepared script – it is a journey into the unexpected.
- A dream character may draw you into some activity or lead off on a path somewhere. You may wish to resist, which could lead

into a discussion as to why. This will bring out the conflict between the inner person and what you think you want. You always have a right to reply. Express your thoughts *and feelings*.

- When the active imagination seems to come to a conclusion or you run out of time, come out of it gently.
- Write down the experience immediately afterwards.
- Spend some time praying about any insights gained and issues raised.

Robert Johnson warns us that during active imagination we must not let one part of ourselves, or archetype, take over at the expense of others. In other words, we cannot sacrifice essential values in order to pursue one narrow goal.[50] Our ego Self must retain autonomy and has an ethical responsibility to uphold human values. Johnson explains,

> In a certain sense, the unconscious is amoral . . . Every archetype, every power, within the collective unconscious, is morally neutral, like the other forces of nature. By itself it cannot put moral or ethical limits on what it does or what it demands. Only human consciousness can take into consideration other values that should be preserved.[51]

Johnson also cautions that we should not use the images of external, physical people known to us in active imagination. This is for two reasons. First, there may be the temptation to take up the active imagination physically when you are with that person next, and second, what we do at the unconscious level is transmitted through the collective unconscious to the unconsciousness of people around us and involuntarily affects them.[52] The way to get around this is to change the appearance of the person in the active imagination, so that external realities do not get confused with our internal energy systems.

A variation on this exercise in active imagination is to *invite Jesus into the dream scene*. This is a method used in the Christian ministry of healing of memories. Accordingly, it would be appropriate to use this where some inner healing is desired. In dreamwork, it entails inviting Jesus into the dream scene rather than a historical memory. (The dream could of course be related to a memory.) This gives the opportunity to bring the healing presence of Christ into our struggles with dream material that contains hurt or confusion. As previously, offer the time to God for his guidance and safe keeping. Then enter into a meditative state and recall the dream. Once it is there in all its facets, invite Jesus into the dream picture and open the dream story to him. You may wish to tell him how you feel in the dream. In your imagination, again without controlling, allow the picture to unfold and give Jesus space to respond. Watch what he says and does. Once the contemplation has drawn to a close, talk to Jesus about how you found the experience and make any resolutions necessary for action. It may be that an act of forgiveness is required or further work on the issue needed. Inner healing is rarely instantaneous; it is very much a process.

Symbol immersion

This again uses the imagination but in a very focused and objective way. It enables us to select and relate to a specific symbol that attracts our attention.[53]

- Still down and enter into a meditative state.
- Enter into the dream scene in your imagination and concentrate on your chosen symbol as it appears uniquely in the dream.
- Examine the symbol and its qualities in as much detail as possible. You may need to change its position or pick it up. The objective is to perceive the symbol as clearly as possible and relate to it.
- Ask yourself: 'How am I now relating to the symbol?' The symbol's energy flows to you from this relationship to bring peace, healing, wisdom, insight, new possibilities – whatever is needed, to be carried into waking life.

An extension to this exercise is then to carry the symbol either backward or forward in time. You may wish to initiate this by asking questions such as: 'How did you get to be here? Where have you come from?' Or, 'Where are you going to from here? How can I begin relating to you to bring about healing or a resolution in my life?' Follow the movement as the symbol regresses or begins to move forward in time. Notice how you relate to each other. When the procedure comes to a natural stopping place, offer gratitude to the symbol and reflect upon what you have learnt.

Using the arts

Narrative writing is not the only way in which a dream can be captured. It can be very enlightening to illustrate the dream in a more creative form: for instance, sketching, painting, sculpture, poetry, music, drama and even dance. What medium we choose may depend on our own particular flair and temperament. However, we should not be put off from trying something new because of our lack of expertise in a certain area. The primary goal is to find expression for the energy of the dream and to see it from a different perspective rather than to produce a great work of art! Do not worry about your professional ability; we all have some innate ability to express images, even if at a primitive level. It may be something that you wish to share with others or keep to yourself. Some people choose to illustrate their dream journals, while others will want more scope to work on than a page in a journal. You might take the dream as a whole or it may be appropriate to choose a particular symbol to work on. To concretize the symbol in an art form can help to make the symbol come fully alive for us and give us something to relate to. Do not be afraid to depict frightening or negative images. It is a way of containing the energy. If you wanted, you could always include a balancing or healing symbol in with it.[54] When you have finished, stand back and regard your artwork and consider what else it has shown you. If it is something tangible, keep it in a special place where you will encounter it frequently. It may continue to produce new insights for you.

Working with others

One to one

It can be immensely helpful to share a dream with someone else. Other people can ask questions and suggest possibilities that we may not have thought of. We all have 'blind spots', certain things that we find difficult to see and accept about ourselves. Sometimes it is useful to have someone else to hold up a mirror! That said, it is essential that the person can be trusted and has some appreciation of dreams. It could be a partner, close friend, spiritual director or therapist. If it is a therapist, then the chances are that they will have a certain level of expertise in this area. As far as spiritual directors are concerned, it would depend upon the individual spiritual director as to how comfortable they felt working with dreams. It is my belief that dreamwork can be a valuable instrument for the ministry of spiritual direction. Regrettably, it is not included in the standard training for spiritual directors. However, there are occasional training days and workshops run by spiritual direction networks on the subject of spiritual direction and dreams.

So let us look at an approach for working with someone else's dream. It is easy to feel a sense of panic when someone has told us a dream they have had and then sits there waiting for us to 'interpret' it. The first step in working with someone else's dream is to recognize that we do not have the answers. However, we can be involved in a process of enquiry and suggestion, which enables the other person to unpack the meaning of the dream. Only they will know when a 'correct' interpretation is arrived at that resonates with them. You do not have to be a qualified psychotherapist or trained counsellor to work with people on their dreams, but you need to be a sensitive and responsible human being. Basic listening skills are a must.[55] The issue of confidentiality is also critical; the person needs to know that they can talk in confidence, that what they reveal will not be gossiped around the church or anywhere else. Dreams reveal our innermost secrets, the treasures of our soul. In telling someone a dream, we make ourselves incredibly vulnerable. Things may come to light that we had not seen previously for ourselves and we need to feel safe with the person with whom we are sharing.

Dreams are taken as direct expressions of the dreamer's unconscious, to be understood in context. The dreamer's life setting, both work and home life, relationships, past history and psychological state will all inform the dreamwork. An image presented will have different associations for each individual, and its network of relationships with the dreamer and his life needs to be unravelled. According to Jung, each symbol should be explored in turn 'by a methodical questioning of the dreamer's own associations'[56] until the meaning for the dreamer is established as closely as possible. We need the dreamer's help to limit the multiple meanings to those that are essential. The dreamer may have certain associations that may be contrary to expectation. For example, to take the motif of a table, we might presume that this is an everyday object associated with meals or work, but the dreamer may have had a disturbing experience relating to this particular table. Dream motifs should not be stereotyped. Jung writes:

> for the purpose of ascertaining the meaning of the dream, I have developed a procedure which I call 'taking up the context'. This consists in making sure that every shade of meaning which each salient feature of the dream has for the dreamer is determined by the associations of the dreamer himself. I therefore proceed in the same way as I would in deciphering a difficult text.[57]

It is, therefore, necessary to work with the dreamer in person. It is impossible to study someone else's dream journal and come up with an 'interpretation' in the absence of the dreamer. The dreamer has to be consulted and be a part of the process. The best way to work with someone else on his or her dreams is face to face. Russ Parker offers a useful framework for working with others on their dreams.[58] However, as it focuses upon feelings only, as opposed to working with symbols, I suggest a method which adapts this framework and incorporates the Jungian perspectives already outlined. In all of this, we need to keep in mind the golden rule: *only the dreamer can interpret the dream.* We may offer insights but it must 'click' with the dreamer him- or herself.

1 Invite the dreamer to relate the dream. Listen without interrupting and ask any questions of clarification at the end. Then reflect back the dream, in a summarized form, using as many of the dreamer's own words as possible and reflecting back in full the dreamer's 'feeling' words. Allowing speakers to hear their own words and feelings coming back at them enables their own work of self-discovery.

2 Ask the dreamer to retell the dream in the present tense (unless this was done in the first instance). This brings it alive and conveys the immediacy of the dream. It cuts down the distance between the dream and the event(s) it relates to. It also helps to connect up with more material within the dream.

3 Continue summarizing and reflecting back, inviting the dreamer to point out any new elements which he or she has become aware of. Make a special note of the feelings contained in the dream. These inform us where the dreamer is living emotionally.

4 Examine the symbols in the dream. For each, get the dreamer to make his or her personal amplifications and associations. Then establish which is most relevant.

5 What is the dreamer's life context? Check out any recent or related events which correspond with the feelings and key symbol associations observed from the dream.

6 Identify the dominant message of the dream for prayer and action.

Depending upon the length of the dream and the amount of time available to work on it, it may be necessary and appropriate to return to the dream on subsequent occasions. The dreamer may find it helps the process to do some individual work on the dream in the interim. There is nothing wrong with the other person putting forward his or her own ideas, so long as the insights continue to be sifted by the dreamer, as the ultimate judge of what is relevant.

Group work

Dreamwork does not have to be carried out on a one to one arrangement. In some areas dream groups have been established. The advantage of a group is that there are more perspectives to be offered on each dream and the dreamer will be exposed to a fuller range of the dream's possible meanings. A disadvantage is the greater level of vulnerability for those who find it difficult opening up in a group context. However, a certain code of practice should have been agreed upon for the group, covering issues such as mutual respect and confidentiality. Everyone is in it together, it is reciprocal – all share and all can offer their wisdom to others. When I was at theological college in Cambridge, I had a brief experience of being part of a dream group facilitated by Madeleine O'Callaghan, a prominent educator in this field who runs her own programme of events.[59] It was a very enlivening experience as we 'unpacked' individual dreams and began to discover more about each other and ourselves. Someone would suggest something that had not occurred to the rest of us, propelling the process forward and sparking off other thoughts. It was like lighting the touch-paper of a fire.

Groups may have a leader who is seen as the 'professional' or they may be lay led. In either case, I think it is helpful to have someone in the role of a facilitator to ensure that appropriate boundaries are maintained, such as time-keeping and directing the discussion so that participants take turns to speak. As with any group work to do with spiritual and emotional sharing, it is helpful to begin with some sort of centring exercise to disengage from outside concerns and be present to the group. Then it is a good idea to go around the circle and let everyone share the dream they have brought, without comment, before selecting dreams to work on. That way at least everyone will have had the chance to share something. It is best for dreams to be read from the journal accounts, so that nothing is repressed or forgotten. Depending on the size of the group and amount of time available, it may be necessary to defer working on some dreams until the next meeting. If this is the case, it is important that in the long run all have a chance to have their dreams worked on fairly. For each session, it should be ensured that the dreams considered have an equal amount of time allocated to each. Dreamwork is inexhaustible and could go on indefinitely if a line is not drawn under it. Hopefully, after an individual dream has been worked on for the set time, the dreamer will have gained some insights to take away. It needs to be remembered that dreams have multiple meanings and so more than one insight could be relevant. Viewpoints should not be pitched against each other.

Each person chosen to have a dream examined should relate it again in the present tense without any interruptions from anyone else. While a dream is being shared, pay attention to it with your whole being, including feelings. Once the dream has been listened to and attended to fully, any questions of clarification about the dream account can be asked, then a course of suggestion and questioning can begin. Jeremy Taylor makes an important point about group dreamwork, that the flashes of insight, the 'ahas', that are felt by those receiving the dream are always a truth about *oneself* and not necessarily a truth about the other person's dream – it may say more about the person making the comment than the dreamer! For this reason, it is useful to preface any remark with 'if it were *my* dream . . .'[60] However, we are not to be too discouraged by this, for 'Even though we can do nothing but project ourselves into the understanding of other people's dreams, these projections often prove to be the source of insight for the dreamer.'[61]

The 'question and comment' dreamwork method tends to be the staple diet for dream groups; however, other techniques such as active imagination may be employed for more established groups. Taylor observes that there can be multiple insights when a group engages in a dramatic presentation of a dream. This is often best done by the dreamer assigning the parts and directing the performance, but that does not need to be the case.[62] Finally, do not be so serious that you lose sight of the fact that group dreamwork is meant to be enjoyable!

Conclusion

There is a need for answers. We do not deny that. But the deepest answers come not out of the dream, nor out of our own ego consciousness, but out of the *active relationship* between ourselves and the Source of the dream.[63]

It is vital to hold in mind, while we wrestle with the 'text' of a dream, that it is not merely an entity in itself to be analysed. The dream is a message from the fount of our very Selves and our Creator. We listen to and dialogue with the source of the wisdom. It is a living, dynamic relationship. As with any relationship, things are not always perfect and we cannot always get everything sewn up in a nice tidy package as swiftly as we would like. To give a biblical perspective, we live in the 'now and the not yet', an in-between time when we can taste the fruits of God's kingdom but everything is not brought to completion in this life. However, God, the divine, or however you want to name the source of creation, accompanies us on our journey and longs that we should discover our true identity in relation to God's Self.

> So lead me
> Lead me through my hopes and fears
> > through the pain of uncried tears
> Lead me to the pinnacle of my potential
> > to the depths of my discernment
> Lead me to consent to be loved
> > and to love.
> Lead me on the path to wholeness.

Notes

Foreword

1 Jeremy Taylor, *Dream Work* (New Jersey: Paulist Press, 1983), p. 225.
2 Francis Bridger and David Atkinson, *Counselling in Context: Developing a Theological Framework* (London: HarperCollins, 1994), p. 51.

Chapter 1

1 Frieda Fordham, *An Introduction to Jung's Psychology* (London: Penguin, 1953), p. 15.
2 Fordham, *An Introduction*, p. 21.
3 Fordham, *An Introduction*, p. 21.
4 Fordham, *An Introduction*, p. 21.
5 Fordham, *An Introduction*, pp. 21–2.
6 Fordham, *An Introduction*, p. 24.
7 C. G. Jung, *The Archetypes and the Collective Unconscious* (London: Routledge and Kegan Paul, 1959), p. 5.
8 Anthony Stevens, *Private Myths: Dreams and Dreaming* (London: Hamish Hamilton, 1995), p. 208.
9 Stevens, *Private Myths*, p. 209.
10 Robert Bly, *A Little Book of the Human Shadow* (San Francisco: HarperSanFrancisco, 1988), p. 17.
11 Brother David Steindl-Rast, 'The Shadow in Christianity', in C. Zweig and J. Abrams (eds), *Meeting the Shadow* (New York: Tarcher/Putnam, 1991), p. 132.
12 Robert Louis Stevenson, *The Strange Case of Dr Jekyll and Mr Hyde* (London: Penguin, 1979), Introduction, p. 9.
13 John A. Sanford, *Dreams: God's Forgotten Language* (New York: HarperCollins, 1968/1989), p. 24.
14 Bishop Richard Harries assesses the justification for the Iraq war in *Church Times*, 9 August 2002.
15 Jennifer Swift, 'Why War Won't Help the Iraqi People', in *Church Times*, 14 March 2003.
16 Rachel Harden, 'Bishops Slam Bush and Blair', in *Church Times*, 2 January 2004.
17 Scripture quotations are from the New Revised Standard Version of the Bible, copyright © 1989 by the Division of Christian Education of the National Council of the Churches of Christ in the USA. Used by permission. All rights reserved.
18 Steindl-Rast, 'The Shadow in Christianity', p. 132.

19 Steindl-Rast, 'The Shadow in Christianity', p. 132.
20 Possibly the work of a late fourteenth-century English priest.
21 Halcyon Backhouse (ed.), *The Cloud of Unknowing* (London: Hodder & Stoughton, 1985), p. 9.
22 Backhouse (ed.), *The Cloud of Unknowing*, pp. 23–4.
23 Stevens, *Private Myths*, pp. 212–13.
24 Stevens, *Private Myths*, p. 210.
25 David Fontana, *The Secret Language of Dreams* (London: Pavilion, 1994), p. 37.
26 Stevens, *Private Myths*, p. 210.
27 Sanford, *Dreams*, pp. 11f.
28 Stevens, *Private Myths*, p. 210.
29 Bly, *Shadow*, p. 18.
30 Stevens, *Private Myths*, p. 208.
31 Stevens, *Private Myths*, p. 139.
32 Stevens, *Private Myths*, p. 209.
33 David Harvey, *The Condition of Postmodernity* (Oxford: Basil Blackwell, 1989), p. 38.
34 Stevens, *Private Myths*, pp. 335–6.
35 Stevens, *Private Myths*, p. 339.
36 Stevens, *Private Myths*, p. 353.
37 Fraser Watts and Mark Williams, *The Psychology of Religious Knowing* (Cambridge: Cambridge University Press, 1988), p. 153.
38 Watts and Williams, *Knowing*, p. 3.
39 Watts and Williams, *Knowing*, p. 95.
40 Ana-Maria Rizzuto, *The Birth of the Living God* (London: University of Chicago Press, 1979), p. 209.
41 Cited by Mark A. Kunkel *et al.*, 'God Images: A Concept Map', *Journal for the Scientific Study of Religion*, 38:2 (1999), pp. 193–4.
42 Watts and Williams, *Knowing*, p. 31.
43 Watts and Williams, *Knowing*, p. 31.
44 John A. Sanford, *Dreams and Healing* (New Jersey: Paulist Press, 1978), p. 102.
45 Sanford, *Dreams*, p. 181.
46 Sanford, *Dreams*, p. 174.
47 Sanford, *Dreams*, pp. 182–3.
48 Sanford, *Dreams*, p. 183.
49 Sanford, *Dreams*, p. 175.

Chapter 2

1 William Shakespeare, *The Complete Works of William Shakespeare* (London: Henry Pordes, 1990), p. 958.
2 Louis M. Savary, P. H. Berne and S. K. Williams, *Dreams and Spiritual Growth* (New Jersey: Paulist Press, 1984), p. 4.

3 David Fontana, *The Secret Language of Dreams* (London: Pavilion, 1994), p. 14; Anthony Stevens, *Private Myths: Dreams and Dreaming* (London: Hamish Hamilton, 1995), p. 87.
4 Stevens, *Private Myths*, pp. 89–90.
5 Fontana, *Dreams*, p. 15.
6 Stevens, *Private Myths*, p. 90.
7 Fontana, *Dreams*, p. 15.
8 Stevens, *Private Myths*, p. 3.
9 Frieda Fordham, *An Introduction to Jung's Psychology* (London: Penguin, 1953), p. 106.
10 Stevens, *Private Myths*, pp. 33–4.
11 Stevens, *Private Myths*, pp. 29–30.
12 Stevens, *Private Myths*, p. 31.
13 Carl G. Jung, *Dreams* (London: Ark, 1982), p. 46.
14 Jung, *Dreams*, p. 73.
15 Jung, *Dreams*, p. 39.
16 Jung, *Dreams*, p. 82.
17 Jung, *Dreams*, p. 36.
18 Jung, *Dreams*, pp. 73–4.
19 Jung, *Dreams*, p. 41.
20 Jung, *Dreams*, p. 42.
21 Jung, *Dreams*, p. 43.
22 Jung, *Dreams*, p. 43.
23 Jung, *Dreams*, p. 45.
24 Jung, *Dreams*, pp. 46–7.
25 Stevens, *Private Myths*, p. 349.
26 Morton Kelsey, *Dreams: A Way to Listen to God* (New York: Paulist Press, 1978), p. 26.
27 Kelsey, *Dreams*, p. 27.
28 Kelsey, *Dreams*, p. 28.
29 Stevens, *Private Myths*, p. 220.
30 Stevens, *Private Myths*, p. 5.
31 Jung, *Dreams*, p. 52.
32 Jung, *Dreams*, p. 53.
33 Jung, *Dreams*, pp. 53–4.
34 Fordham, *An Introduction*, pp. 101–2.
35 Jung, *Dreams*, p. 76.
36 Robert A. Johnson, *Inner Work* (San Francisco, CA: Harper & Row, 1986), p. 27.
37 Stevens, *Private Myths*, p. 4.
38 Stevens, *Private Myths*, p. 130.
39 Jung, *Dreams*, p. 77.
40 Fontana, *Dreams*, p. 35.
41 Fontana, *Dreams*, p. 35.
42 Stevens, *Private Myths*, p. 4.

43 Johnson, *Inner Work*, p. 49.
44 Jung, *Dreams*, p. 78.
45 Stevens, *Private Myths*, p. 155.
46 Stevens, *Private Myths*, p. 154.
47 Stevens, *Private Myths*, p. 146.
48 Jung, *Dreams*, p. 34.
49 Stevens, *Private Myths*, p. 148.
50 Jung, *Dreams*, pp. 80ff.
51 Stevens, *Private Myths*, p. 134.
52 Johnson, *Inner Work*, p. 29.
53 John A. Sanford, *Dreams: God's Forgotten Language* (New York: HarperCollins, 1968/1989), p. 105.
54 Stevens, *Private Myths*, p. 210.
55 Kathrin Asper, *The Inner Child in Dreams* (Boston and London: Shambhala, 1992), p. 48.
56 Stevens, *Private Myths*, p. 136.
57 Johnson, *Inner Work*, p. 27.
58 Johnson, *Inner Work*, p. 28.
59 Cited by Johnson, *Inner Work*, p. 28.
60 Stevens, *Private Myths*, p. 52.
61 Fontana, *Dreams*, p. 34.
62 Johnson, *Inner Work*, p. 28.
63 Jung, *Dreams*, p. 79.
64 Stevens, *Private Myths*, p. 131.
65 Stevens, *Private Myths*, pp. 129–30.
66 Johnson, *Inner Work*, p. 30.
67 Fontana, *Dreams*, pp. 36–8.
68 Fontana, *Dreams*, p. 34.
69 Johnson, *Inner Work*, p. 33.

Chapter 3

1 John R. Kohlenberger and Edward W. Goodrick, *The NIV Complete Concordance* (London: Hodder & Stoughton, 1988).
2 Louis M. Savary, P. H. Berne and S. K. Williams, *Dreams and Spiritual Growth* (New Jersey: Paulist Press, 1984), pp. 38, 50.
3 Savary *et al.*, *Dreams*, p. 51.
4 Savary *et al.*, *Dreams*, p. 52.
5 Savary *et al.*, *Dreams*, p. 53.
6 Russ Parker, *Dream Stories* (Oxford: Bible Reading Fellowship, 2002), p. 14.
7 Seymour Rossel, *Bible Dreams: The Spiritual Quest* (New York: SIP Books, 2003), pp. 256–7.
8 Gordon Wenham, *Word Biblical Commentary: Genesis 16–50* (Dallas: Word, 1994), pp. 390–1.

9 Wenham, *Genesis 16–50*, p. 390.
10 Kenneth McLeish, *Myths and Legends of the World* (London: Bloomsbury, 1996), pp. 59–60.
11 Wenham, *Genesis 16–50*, p. 391.
12 Rossel, *Bible Dreams*, pp. 259–61.
13 Wenham, *Genesis 16–50*, p. 391.
14 Wenham, *Genesis 16–50*, p. 393.
15 Parker, *Dream Stories*, p. 38.
16 John E. Goldingay, *Word Biblical Commentary: Daniel* (Dallas: Word, 1987), p. 92.
17 Goldingay, *Daniel*, p. 92.
18 Savary *et al.*, *Dreams*, p. 28.
19 Savary *et al.*, *Dreams*, p. 29.

Chapter 4

1 Carl G. Jung, *Dreams* (London: Ark, 1982), p. 68.
2 Carl G. Jung, 'Approaching the Unconscious', in *Man and his Symbols* (London: Picador, 1978), p. 27.
3 Jeremy Taylor, *Where People Fly and Water Runs Uphill* (New York: Warner Books, 1992), pp. 205–6.
4 Anthony Stevens, *Private Myths: Dreams and Dreaming* (London: Hamish Hamilton, 1995), p. 13.
5 Jung, 'Unconscious', in *Symbols*, p. 36.
6 Jung, 'Unconscious', p. 27.
7 Jung, 'Unconscious', p. 28.
8 Jung, 'Unconscious', p. 29.
9 Jung, 'Unconscious', p. 34.
10 Jung, 'Unconscious', p. 37.
11 Jeremy Taylor, *Dream Work* (New Jersey: Paulist Press, 1983), p. 128.
12 Jung, 'Unconscious', pp. 29, 33.
13 Stevens, *Private Myths*, p. 176.
14 Stevens, *Private Myths*, p. 177.
15 Jung, 'Unconscious', p. 41.
16 Stevens, *Private Myths*, pp. 178–9.
17 Carl G. Jung, *The Archetypes and the Collective Unconscious* (London: Routledge and Kegan Paul, 1959), p. 8.
18 Jung, *Archetypes*, p. 15.
19 Jung, *Archetypes*, p. 23.
20 Jung, *Archetypes*, p. 24.
21 Stevens, *Private Myths*, p. 182.
22 Louis M. Savary, P. H. Berne and S. K. Williams, *Dreams and Spiritual Growth* (New Jersey: Paulist Press, 1984), p. 144.
23 Jung, 'Unconscious', p. 4.
24 Taylor, *Dream Work*, pp. 35, 40–1.

25 Jung, 'Unconscious', p. 38.

26 Kathrin Asper, *The Inner Child in Dreams* (Boston and London: Shambhala, 1992), p. 23.

27 Taylor, *Dream Work*, p. 136.

28 Jung, 'Unconscious', p. 42.

29 Such as: J. E. Cirlot, *A Dictionary of Symbols* (New York: Dover Publications, 2002).

30 Jung, *Dreams*, pp. 33, 72–3; Jung, 'Unconscious', p. 38.

31 Jung, *Dreams*, p. 69; Jung, 'Unconscious', p. 38.

32 Jung, 'Unconscious', p. 40.

33 Taylor, *Dream Work*, p. 119.

34 Robert Johnson, *Inner Work* (San Francisco, CA: Harper & Row, 1986), p. 78.

35 Carl G. Jung, *Memories, Dreams, Reflections* (London: Fontana Press, 1993), pp. 182–3.

36 Jung, 'Unconscious', p. 43.

37 Johnson, *Inner Work*, p. 79.

38 David Fontana, *The Secret Language of Dreams* (London: Pavilion, 1994), p. 135.

39 Stevens, *Private Myths*, p. 193.

40 Jung, *Archetypes*, p. 18.

41 Jung, *Archetypes*, pp. 18–19.

42 Jung, *Archetypes*, p. 20.

43 Jung, *Archetypes*, p. 21.

44 Jung, 'Unconscious', p. 15.

45 Taylor, *Dream Work*, p. 145.

46 See Freud's interpretation of Jung's dream in Jung, *Memories, Dreams, Reflections*, p. 183.

47 Taylor, *Dream Work*, p. 65.

48 Taylor, *Dream Work*, p. 67.

49 Taylor, *Dream Work*, p. 67.

50 Taylor, *Dream Work*, p. 68.

51 Gilles Néret, *Dali* (Koln: Evergreen, 1996), pp. 74–5 and 'The Image of Christ' in G. Finaldi (ed.), *The Image of Christ: The Catalogue of the Exhibition 'Seeing Salvation'* (London: National Gallery, 2000).

52 Johnson, *Inner Work*, p. 49.

53 John A. Sanford, *Dreams and Healing* (New Jersey: Paulist Press, 1978), p. 24.

54 Jung, *Archetypes*, p. 22; Taylor, *Dream Work*, p. 152.

55 Jung, *Archetypes*, p. 38.

56 Jung, *Dreams*, p. 115.

57 Savary *et al.*, *Dreams*, p. 132.

58 Stevens, *Private Myths*, pp. 217–18.

59 Johnson, *Inner Work*, p. 49; Stevens, *Private Myths*, p. 217.

60 Jung, *Archetypes*, p. 355.

61 Jung, *Archetypes*, p. 357.
62 Taylor, *Dream Work*, p. 156.
63 Taylor, *Dream Work*, p. 155.
64 Taylor, *Dream Work*, p. 159.
65 Taylor, *Dream Work*, p. 159.
66 Jung, *Archetypes*, p. 29.
67 Jung, *Archetypes*, pp. 26–7.
68 Jung, *Archetypes*, p. 66.
69 Jung, *Archetypes*, p. 28.
70 Jung, *Archetypes*, p. 27.
71 John A. Sanford, *The Invisible Partners: How the Male and Female in Each of Us Affects our Relationships* (New Jersey: Paulist Press, 1980), p. 13.
72 Sanford, *Invisible Partners*, p. 13.
73 Sanford, *Invisible Partners*, p. 15.
74 Taylor, *Dream Work*, p. 164.
75 Sanford, *Invisible Partners*, pp. 15–16.
76 Sanford, *Invisible Partners*, pp. 16–17.
77 Sanford, *Invisible Partners*, pp. 72–3.
78 Sanford, *Invisible Partners*, pp. 77–8.
79 Taylor, *Dream Work*, p. 165.
80 Jung, *Archetypes*, p. 255.
81 Jung, 'Unconscious', pp. 107ff.
82 Jung, *Archetypes*, p. 256.
83 Jung, *Archetypes*, p. 35.
84 Taylor, *Dream Work*, p. 171.
85 Taylor, *Dream Work*, pp. 166–7.
86 St John of the Cross, quoted in Elizabeth Ruth, *Lamps of Fire: Daily Readings with St John of the Cross* (London: Darton, Longman and Todd, 1985), p. 3.

Chapter 5

1 Anthony Stevens, *Private Myths: Dreams and Dreaming* (London: Hamish Hamilton, 1995), p. 156.
2 John A. Sanford, *Dreams and Healing* (New Jersey: Paulist Press, 1978), p. 5.
3 Louis M. Savary, P. H. Berne and S. K. Williams, *Dreams and Spiritual Growth* (New Jersey: Paulist Press, 1984), p. 132.
4 Savary *et al.*, *Dreams*, p. 70.
5 Savary *et al.*, *Dreams*, p. 70.
6 Savary *et al.*, *Dreams*, p. 103.
7 Savary *et al.*, *Dreams*, p. 113.
8 Sanford, *Dreams and Healing*, p. 99.
9 Sanford, *Dreams and Healing*, p. 100.

10 Sanford, *Dreams and Healing*, p. 99.
11 Sanford, *Dreams and Healing*, p. 100.
12 Sanford, *Dreams and Healing*, pp. 100–1.
13 Sanford, *Dreams and Healing*, p. 101.
14 Dennis and Matthew Linn, *Healing Life's Hurts* (New York: Paulist Press, 1978), p. 209.
15 Stevens, *Private Myths*, p. 198.
16 Stevens, *Private Myths*, p. 199.
17 Stevens, *Private Myths*, p. 165.
18 Sanford, *Dreams and Healing*, p. 34.
19 Sanford, *Dreams and Healing*, pp. 36–7.
20 Sanford, *Dreams and Healing*, p. 40.
21 Sanford, *Dreams and Healing*, p. 34.
22 Stevens, *Private Myths*, pp. 253–6.
23 Linn, *Life's Hurts*, p. 11.
24 Linn, *Life's Hurts*, p. 205.
25 Kathrin Asper, *The Inner Child in Dreams* (Boston and London: Shambhala, 1992), Preface.
26 Asper, *Inner Child*, p. 5.
27 Asper, *Inner Child*, p. 48.
28 Asper, *Inner Child*, p. 25.
29 Asper, *Inner Child*, pp. 97–8.
30 Asper, *Inner Child*, p. 33.
31 Asper, *Inner Child*, p. 55.
32 Asper, *Inner Child*, p. 60.
33 Asper, *Inner Child*, pp. 62–7.
34 Asper, *Inner Child*, p. 67.
35 Asper, *Inner Child*, p. 67.
36 Asper, *Inner Child*, p. 68.
37 Asper, *Inner Child*, pp. 52–3.
38 Jeremy Taylor, *Dream Work* (New Jersey: Paulist Press, 1983), p. 176.
39 Asper, *Inner Child*, pp. 96–7.
40 Asper, *Inner Child*, pp. 102–3.
41 Asper, *Inner Child*, p. 76.
42 Gilles Néret, *Dali* (Koln: Evergreen, 1996), p. 26.
43 Jeremy Taylor, *Where People Fly and Water Runs Uphill* (New York: Warner Books, 1992), p. 31.
44 Taylor, *Where People Fly*, pp. 32–4.
45 Stevens, *Private Myths*, pp. 279ff.
46 Carl G. Jung, *Man and his Symbols* (London: Picador, 1989), p. 36.
47 Jung cited by Stevens, *Private Myths*, p. 273.
48 Carl G. Jung, *Dreams* (London: Ark, 1982), p. 48.
49 Taylor, *Dream Work*, p. 123.
50 Taylor, *Dream Work*, p. 125.
51 Taylor, *Dream Work*, p. 123.

52 Robert A. Johnson, *Inner Work* (San Francisco, CA: Harper & Row, 1986), pp. 48–9.
53 Johnson, *Inner Work*, p. 49.
54 Sanford, *Dreams and Healing*, pp. 37–9.
55 Jung, *Dreams*, pp. 75–6.
56 Carl G. Jung, *The Archetypes and the Collective Unconscious* (London: Routledge and Kegan Paul, 1959), pp. 17f.
57 Savary *et al.*, *Dreams*, p. 129.
58 Savary *et al.*, *Dreams*, p. 133.
59 *Church Times*, 17 September 2004.

Chapter 6

1 Carl G. Jung, *Dreams* (London: Ark, 1982), p. 69.
2 Jung, *Dreams*, p. 72.
3 Jung, *Dreams*, 69.
4 Russ Parker, *Healing Dreams* (London: Triangle SPCK, 1993), pp. 82–4.
5 Jung, *Dreams*, p. 25.
6 Kathrin Asper, *The Inner Child in Dreams* (Boston and London: Shambhala, 1992), p. 12.
7 Michael Leunig, 'A Common Prayer', in *Common Prayer Collection* (London: Collins Dove, 1993).
8 Jeremy Taylor, *Dream Work* (New Jersey: Paulist Press, 1983), p. 43.
9 Taylor, *Dream Work*, p. 48.
10 Refer to books on contemplative prayer. Jim Borst, *Coming to God in the Stillness* (Stowmarket: Kevin Mayhew, 2004) in the *Exploring Prayer* series is a good starter.
11 Jim Cotter, *Prayer at Night* (Sheffeld: Cairns Publishers, 1991), p. 55.
12 Madeleine O'Callaghan workshop at Ridley Hall, Cambridge; see p. 132.
13 Anthony Stevens, *Private Myths: Dreams and Dreaming* (London: Hamish Hamilton, 1995), p. 56.
14 Louis M. Savary, P. H. Berne and S. K. Williams, *Dreams and Spiritual Growth* (New Jersey: Paulist Press, 1984), p. 78.
15 Robert A. Johnson, *Inner Work* (San Francisco, CA: Harper & Row, 1986), pp. 59–60.
16 Johnson, *Inner Work*, p. 61.
17 Savary *et al.*, *Dreams*, p. 79.
18 Johnson, *Inner Work*, p. 63.
19 Johnson, *Inner Work*, p. 56.
20 Johnson, *Inner Work*, p. 56.
21 Johnson, *Inner Work*, p. 66.
22 Johnson, *Inner Work*, p. 70.
23 Johnson, *Inner Work*, p. 76.
24 Johnson, *Inner Work*, pp. 76–7.

25 Johnson, *Inner Work*, p. 64.
26 Johnson, *Inner Work*, pp. 72, 75.
27 Johnson, *Inner Work*, p. 73.
28 Jung, *Dreams*, p. 102.
29 Stevens, *Private Myths*, p. 57.
30 Johnson, *Inner Work*, pp. 87–8.
31 Johnson, *Inner Work*, p. 90.
32 Johnson, *Inner Work*, p. 90.
33 Johnson, *Inner Work*, pp. 94ff.
34 Johnson, *Inner Work*, p. 96.
35 Johnson, *Inner Work*, p. 97.
36 Johnson, *Inner Work*, p. 100.
37 Johnson, *Inner Work*, p. 102.
38 Johnson, *Inner Work*, p. 99.
39 Refer to Jonny Baker, Doug Gay and Jenny Brown, *Alternative Worship* (London: SPCK, 2003).
40 Johnson, *Inner Work*, p. 102.
41 Savary *et al.*, *Dreams*, p. 57.
42 Russ Parker, *Healing Dreams*, p. 22.
43 Savary *et al.*, *Dreams*, p. 57.
44 Based upon Savary *et al.*, Dreamwork Technique 5, *Dreams*, pp. 62f.
45 Savary *et al.*, *Dreams*, p. 58.
46 Savary *et al.*, *Dreams*, p. 57.
47 Johnson, *Inner Work*, p. 171.
48 Johnson, *Inner Work*, p. 140.
49 Johnson, *Inner Work*, pp. 186–7.
50 Johnson, *Inner Work*, p. 192.
51 Johnson, *Inner Work*, pp. 193–4.
52 Johnson, *Inner Work*, pp. 197–8.
53 Based on Savary *et al.*, *Dreams*, pp. 73–7.
54 Savary *et al.*, *Dreams*, p. 150.
55 There are courses available, such as the one run by the Acorn Christian Healing Foundation; details from the Acorn Christian Foundation, Whitehill Chase, Bordon, Hampshire GU35 OAP.
56 Jung, *Dreams*, p. 71.
57 Jung, *Dreams*, pp. 71–2.
58 Parker, *Healing Dreams*, pp. 83ff.
59 For further information apply to: Madeleine O'Callaghan, 42 Peverel Road, Cambridge CB8 8RH.
60 Taylor, *Dream Work*, p. 83.
61 Taylor, *Dream Work*, pp. 83–4.
62 Taylor, *Dream Work*, p. 88.
63 Savary *et al.*, *Dreams*, p. 23.

Bibliography

Asper, Kathrin, *The Inner Child in Dreams*, Shambhala, Boston and London, 1992.

Backhouse, Halcyon (ed.), *The Cloud of Unknowing*, Hodder & Stoughton, London, 1985.

Baker, Jonny, Gay, Doug and Brown, Jenny, *Alternative Worship*, SPCK, London, 2003.

Bly, Robert, *A Little Book of the Human Shadow*, HarperSanFrancisco, San Francisco, 1988.

Bridger, Francis and Atkinson, David, *Counselling in Context: Developing a Theological Framework*, HarperCollins, London, 1994.

Campbell, Joseph, *The Hero with a Thousand Faces*, Princeton University Press, Princeton, 1990.

Cirlot, J. E., *A Dictionary of Symbols*, Dover Publications, New York, 2002.

Cotter, Jim, *Prayer at Night*, Cairns Publications, Sheffield, 1991.

Finaldi, G. (ed.), *The Image of Christ: The Catalogue of the Exhibition 'Seeing Salvation'*, National Gallery, London, 2000.

Fontana, David, *The Secret Language of Dreams*, Pavilion, London, 1994.

Fordham, Frieda, *An Introduction to Jung's Psychology*, Penguin, London, 1953.

Goldingay, John E., *Word Biblical Commentary: Daniel*, Word, Dallas, 1987.

Griffin, Joseph, *The Origin of Dreams*, The Therapist Ltd, Worthing, 1997.

Harvey, David, *The Condition of Postmodernity*, Basil Blackwell, Oxford, 1989.

Johnson, Robert, A., *Inner Work*, Harper & Row, San Francisco, 1986.

Jung, Carl G., *The Archetypes and the Collective Unconscious*, Routledge and Kegan Paul, London, 1959.

Jung, Carl G., *Man and his Symbols*, Picador, London, 1978.

Jung, Carl G., *Dreams*, Ark, London, 1982.

Jung, Carl G., *Memories, Dreams, Reflections*, Fontana Press, London, 1993.

Kelsey, Morton, *Dreams: A Way to Listen to God*, Paulist Press, New York, 1978.

Kohlenberger, John R. and Goodrick, Edward W., *The NIV Complete Concordance*, Hodder & Stoughton, London, 1988.

Kunkel, Mark A. *et al.*, 'God Images: A Concept Map', *Journal for the Scientific Study of Religion*, 38:2 (1999), 193–202.

Lamont, Gordon, *The Creative Path*, Azure, London, 2004.

Leunig, Michael, 'A Common Prayer', in *Common Prayer Collection*, Collins Dove, New York, 1993.

Linn, Dennis and Linn, Matthew, *Healing Life's Hurts*, Paulist Press, New York, 1978.

McLeish, Kenneth, *Myths and Legends of the World*, Bloomsbury, London, 1996.

Néret, Gilles, *Dali*, Evergreen, Koln, 1996.

Parker, Russ, *Healing Dreams*, Triangle SPCK, London, 1993.

Parker, Russ, *Dream Stories*, Bible Reading Fellowship, Oxford, 2002.

Rizzuto, Ana-Maria, *The Birth of the Living God*, University of Chicago Press, London, 1979.

Rossel, Seymour, *Bible Dreams: The Spiritual Quest*, SPI Books, New York, 2003.

Ruth, Elizabeth, ODC, *Lamps of Fire: Daily Readings with St John of the Cross*, Darton, Longman and Todd, London, 1985.

Samuels, Andrew (ed.), *The Father: Contemporary Jungian Perspectives*, Free Association Books, London, 1985.

Sanford, John A., *Dreams and Healing*, Paulist Press, New Jersey, 1978.

Sanford, John A., *The Invisible Partners: How the Male and Female in Each of Us Affects our Relationships*, Paulist Press, New Jersey, 1980.

Sanford, John A., *Dreams: God's Forgotten Language*, HarperCollins, New York, 1968/1989.

Savary, Louis M., Berne, P. H. and Williams, S. K., *Dreams and Spiritual Growth*, Paulist Press, New Jersey, 1984.

Shakespeare, William, *The Complete Works of William Shakespeare*, edited by W. J. Craig, Henry Pordes, London, 1990.

Steindl-Rast, Brother David, 'The Shadow in Christianity', in C. Zweig and J. Abrams (eds), *Meeting the Shadow*, Tarcher/Putnam, New York, 1991.

Stevens, Anthony, *Private Myths: Dreams and Dreaming*, Hamish Hamilton, London, 1995.

Stevenson, Robert Louis, *The Strange Case of Dr Jekyll and Mr Hyde*, Penguin, London, 1979.

Taylor, Jeremy, *Dream Work*, Paulist Press, New Jersey, 1983.

Taylor, Jeremy, *Where People Fly and Water Runs Uphill*, Warner Books, New York, 1992.

Watts, Fraser and Williams, Mark, *The Psychology of Religious Knowing*, Cambridge University Press, Cambridge, 1988.

Wenham, Gordon, *Word Biblical Commentary: Genesis 16–50*, Word, USA, 1994.

On tape

Johnson, Robert, *Understanding Dream Language*, Dove Entertainment, New York, 1985.

Index